GOVERNOR DUMMER ACADEMY
HISTORY

LIEUTENANT GOVERNOR WILLIAM DUMMER

GOVERNOR DUMMER ACADEMY

HISTORY

1763 - 1963

John W. Ragle

Published by

GOVERNOR DUMMER ACADEMY

SOUTH BYFIELD, MASSACHUSETTS

1963

NEWBURYPORT PRESS, INC.
1963

FOREWORD

When the first settlers began to open up the New England wilderness, their primary concern was for self-preservation and for the creation of a community in which to nurture their religious convictions. Indeed, it is entirely natural that they should have thought first of their safety and physical needs, and in terms of their spiritual well-being. It is not surprising, therefore, that formal education had to be satisfied with a somewhat lower priority.

That our forefathers recognized, nevertheless, the importance of educated men to the ultimate success of the settlements is witnessed to by the founding of Harvard College in 1636 and the establishment in the same year of the Boston Latin School, certainly for the purpose of preparing boys to enter the College. Yet these, together with the Latin school started in Newtowne (Cambridge) shortly afterward, were almost the only educational oases in the area for many years.

In 1647 the General Court of the Massachusetts colony passed a measure requiring that every community of 100 families or more set up its own "grammar" school. Yet the statute, even though armed with a punitive clause, was relatively ineffective. Dr. Claude M. Fuess, a trustee of Governor Dummer Academy, writes in the notes for his forthcoming book, *American Independent Schools and Schoolmasters:*

> For more than a century and a quarter after the colonization of New England, education was in a state of confusion, with no broad pattern discernible. So far as the towns were concerned, it was each community for itself, and the variations in efficiency were very wide. While the General Court tried more than once to impose its authority, the results were far from uniform or satisfactory.

As late as 1840 there were only 18 public schools in Massachusetts! Long before this New Englanders had become aware that provisions for public education were developing far too slowly. They had turned, therefore, to the private academy, which could be supported independently by interested groups or individuals. Independent of the whim of an entire community, such schools had the added advantage of being able to develop freely in those directions which best served the needs they were created to fill. In 1840 the Commonwealth of Massachusetts had 114 private academies.

The academy established at Byfield by the foresight of Colonial Lieutenant Governor William Dummer in 1763 was the first boys' boarding school in this country. Here were trained the men who gave further impetus to the independent school movement, first in Andover, Massachusetts, and shortly thereafter at Exeter, New Hampshire. That Governor Dummer's new academy filled a need widely felt in the days of its founding shall be amply demonstrated in the following pages. What it represents in the face of an equal challenge today is the business of a later section of this history.

J. W. R.

PREFACE

It was early in the summer of 1956 that, at the request of the Board of Trustees of Governor Dummer Academy, I began work on this *History*. From the start, encouragement and helpful suggestions have been forthcoming. This has been particularly the case with Dr. Claude M. Fuess and Dr. Edward W. Eames, without whose guidance I would many times have been in difficulty. It was easy for me to agree to undertake the *History* of a school about to achieve its 200th birthday, a school which dated from prior to the founding of our nation. The first problem came in deciding how the story should be told. This book is the fruit of that decision: it does not purport to be a scholarly work, painstakingly annotated; on the contrary, its primary purpose is to catch the spirit of the Academy in the various periods of its history, and to do this through characterization and anecdote. Nevertheless, in the course of the story nothing will be found for which there is not sound historical evidence.

With the exception of an occasional school vacation, the work on this book has been done during ten-week periods of the summer. This process has had its shortcomings, for it has meant sorting out and picking up the threads each year, after many months spent away from the project. I wish to thank sincerely the Board of Trustees of the Academy, and its representatives — Dr. Eames; Dr. Fuess; its President, Mr. Marshall B. Dalton; and most recently the new Headmaster, Mr. Valleau Wilkie, Jr. — for their unending patience and understanding.

Though a considerable portion of the material for this history has come from the collections of the Essex Institute in Salem, the Harvard University Archives, the Boston Athenaeum, and the Newburyport Public Library, most of it has been found in the Governor Dummer Academy Archives. For this reason, whatever merits this *History* may possess redound in very large part to the credit of the late James M. Barriskill, without whose insight and interest it would not exist.

An antiquarian by vocation, Mr. Barriskill devoted himself, during his eleven years as a teacher at the Academy, to the order-

VII

ing and the expanding of the school's collection of memorabilia. With the erection of the Frost Library and Science Building, he arranged and with great care catalogued the newly provided archives. Finally, I am indebted to him not only for the wealth of ordered material which he laid before me and for the guidance and encouragement which he never failed to provide, but especially for his detailed knowledge of Master Moody (of whom he had made a special and exhaustive study) and of this great first teacher's years at the school.

In the course of my work on this project, aid and information have been freely offered to me wherever I have turned. Mr. Edgar Dunning, the Business Manager of the Academy, as well as all the members of the famous "Old Guard" of the faculty, have provided invaluable support. Miss Louise Lovell, for over twenty years secretary to the office of Headmaster, has with great patience made available many pertinent records, but beyond this has given added insight through her own remembrances. Indeed, the entire office staff of the Academy has been unfailingly cooperative.

I cannot here acknowledge all of the assistance that has been forthcoming from so many friends, many of them alumni, of the school. To all — named or unnamed — my deepest appreciation. Even as this book reaches completion, I am aware of pertinent and yet untapped sources, of others who have reason to know of the history of Governor Dummer. I can only hope that what is represented in the *History* is as accurate and as comprehensive as I believe it to be.

Finally, I must thank sincerely the Board of Trustees of Governor Dummer Academy for giving me the privilege of writing the history of their school.

J. W. R.

TABLE OF CONTENTS

Chapter

LIST OF ILLUSTRATIONS

PROLOGUE

The first decade of the nineteenth century occupies a vital position in the history of the growth and development of the United States of America. As it opened the young Republic had been functioning under its new constitution for scarcely a dozen years. The twelve-year supremacy of the Federalists under George Washington, John Adams, and Alexander Hamilton — which by the establishment of wise precedents had in the midst of controversy given a newly independent people a sound and orderly government — was drawing to an end. Responsibility for the destinies of this energetic young nation was about to descend on the shoulders of the idealistic and democratic leader of the Republican group, Thomas Jefferson. In the next ten years, with the leadership of Jefferson and James Madison, the United States was destined to grow vastly in size, in experience, and in significance among the nations of the world. This was a period fraught with challenge — and attended by perils at home and abroad. It was a period during which the new nation must chart for itself a pathway to security and prestige. Such a time required in all walks of life men of foresight, initiative, and courage.

What is the function of education if it be not to produce such men?

Such a man was Senator Rufus King of Massachusetts and New York, able and eloquent delegate to the Constitutional Convention at Philadelphia, an original signer of the Constitution. He was four times elected to the Senate of the young Republic and at the opening of the nineteenth century was appointed by George Washington to be minister plenipotentiary to Great Britain, from whom the Colonies had so recently won their freedom. At a critical time in her history, Rufus King employed brilliant diplomacy at the court of his country's deposed oppressor. Although later twice defeated as candidate for the Vice-Presidency of the United States and the defeated Federalist candidate for the Presidency in 1816, King served his country in key positions until his death. In the words of Daniel Webster, certainly no mean judge of such talents: "You never heard such a speaker. In strength and dignity, and fire; in ease, in natural effect, and gesture as well as in matter, he is unequalled."

Likewise a member of the Congress of the United States at the outset of the new century, serving his second term, was another able leader. Great-grandson of the first famous Chief Justice of the Massachusetts Supreme Court, Samuel Sewall was himself destined to occupy the seat of his famed ancestor. Furthermore, the man whom in 1813 he was to succeed was the universally admired and respected Theophilus Parsons of Byfield, Massachusetts.

This Theophilus Parsons was a remarkably versatile man. (It is said that as wide a variety of craftsmen as blacksmiths, carpenters, and painters assumed from his informal conversations that he was of their trades.) He had a profound influence on the development of the judiciary system in this country and indirectly played an important part in the drafting of the federal Bill of Rights. At his office in Newburyport studied many of the most promising young lawyers of the day, including John Quincy Adams, sixth President of the United States. Parsons' appointment as Chief Justice in the Supreme Court of the Commonwealth of Massachusetts came in 1806.

The same President Washington who appointed Rufus King his minister to Great Britain had previously selected as his first Postmaster General another Massachusetts man, Samuel Osgood of Andover. Also a former delegate to the Continental Congress, Osgood was in 1803 designated by President Jefferson naval officer to the Port of New York.

While America was developing and setting into motion her intricate domestic mechanism at home, her fast-growing merchant fleet was suffering harassment on the seas. Following the close of hostilities between France and the United States in 1800, British naval vessels continued impressment of American seamen under the guise of reclaiming deserters from their own fleet. And in the Mediterranean Barbary pirates exacted tribute from merchant vessels. Outstanding among the American naval heroes of the day was Commodore Edward Preble, who aboard his famous flagship *Constitution* in 1803 assumed command of the historic campaign against the raiders' headquarters at Tripoli.

On the spot as American consul general in Algiers at this same time was the able and ardent patriot Tobias Lear. For many years private secretary to and close friend and confidant of George Washington, Lear had already distinguished himself (during his

XIV

consulship in the strife-torn Dominican Republic) as a skillful representative of his country. It was he who ultimately negotiated with Tripoli the treaty which was accepted by his government.

Far to the East another American-born leader was, by dint of almost incredible achievements, carving a name for himself both as a soldier and as a statesman. In October, 1804, David Ochterlony, then British Resident at the court of Shah Alam, Emperor of Hindustan, with a bare handful of men stood off until relieved by a British army an enemy force of 20,000 men and 100 guns beseiging Delhi. A magnificent tactician (later a major-general), Sir David Ochterlony did as much as any one man to stabilize the position of the British in India. For years superintendent of the internal affairs of the whole of Central India, Ochterlony proved himself as able an administrator of civil affairs as of military.

Clearly America was producing at this crucial time in her infancy, leaders in all fields of endeavor. A large part of the credit for this must go to the scattered educational centers of the day. (About one-half of the fifty-five delegates to the Constitutional Convention at Independence Hall were college graduates, a remarkable percentage for that day.) In the forefront of the educational scene was, of course, Harvard College in Cambridge, Massachusetts. For almost two centuries she had been training leaders. One of them, Samuel Phillips of Andover, had by 1800 already been the guiding spirit behind the founding of two outstanding private academies, Phillips Academy in Andover, Massachusetts, and Phillips Exeter Academy in New Hampshire. Resourceful and energetic, during the Revolution he had, starting from scratch, developed a powder mill to supply with much-needed ammunition the hard-pressed armies of General Washington. In 1801 he climaxed a remarkable life of service by winning election to the post of Lieutenant-Governor of Massachusetts.

Meanwhile, the President of Harvard College was Joseph Willard. The three most important professorships on his faculty, excluding the medical department, were held by David Tappan, Hollis Professor of Divinity; Eliphalet Pearson, Hancock Professor of Hebrew and Oriental Languages; and Samuel Webber, Hollis Professor of Mathematics and Natural Philosophy. Upon Willard's death in 1804 Professor Pearson, a Fellow of the College (which group also included Theophilus Parsons), was to become Acting President. Already he had cooperated with Samuel Phillips in the establishment of Phillips Academy, and later he was to be instrumental in the founding of the Andover Theological Seminary. Professor Webber was to become in 1806 the fourteenth President of Harvard College.

Rufus King, Samuel Sewall, Theophilus Parsons, Samuel Osgood, Edward Preble, Tobias Lear, David Ochterlony, Samuel Phillips, David Tappan, Eliphalet Pearson, and Samuel Webber were outstanding leaders all. Counted among them were statesmen, jurists, soldiers, diplomats, businessmen, divines, and educators. Within the first decade of the nineteenth century practically all of them played an important role in contributing to the growth in strength and wisdom of their new nation. This they had in common — but something else, too.

For each of these men had in his youth gone to the Dummer School in the parish of Byfield in Massachusetts. There they had studied under the famous and eccentric Master Samuel Moody, the first Preceptor of the school. Indeed, in that first decade of the nineteenth century three of the great man's former students performed the duties of President of the most celebrated college in America. (Joseph Willard, too, had studied under Master Moody before the latter's removal to Byfield.) Three occupied the major professorships of the institution; two were Fellows; and, in addition, two others served as Tutors and another as Librarian. Thus Dummer School at its outset produced leaders that were so important to the initial stages of American independence, including sixteen members of Congress, five of whom were in the Senate. It is upon the history of this venerable institution, established in 1763, prior to the Revolutionary War, that we are now embarked.

GOVERNOR DUMMER ACADEMY

HISTORY

CHAPTER I

The Dummer Family in America

Every evidence emphasizes the fact that Master Moody, though eccentric, and mercurial in temperament, was a gifted teacher and leader of boys. The procuring of his services as first Master of Governor Dummer's school was an act of sheer inspiration. No administration in the long history of the school stands higher in success; very few can claim to approach its achievement; only two or three can justifiably claim to equal it. Credit for acquiring the services of this unique and most interesting eighteenth century schoolmaster belongs to a special committee headed by Moses Parsons, the eminent divine who was for thirty-nine years minister to Byfield Parish. (Reference has already been made to his famous son, the celebrated jurist, scholar, and patriot, Theophilus Parsons.)

The original authority for the Reverend Mr. Parsons to work conjointly with five freeholders — principal inhabitants of Byfield Parish, chosen yearly for that purpose at the annual meeting — derived directly from the last Will and Testament of colonial Lieutenant-Governor William Dummer. From the remarkable benevolence of this far-sighted man stems the school which bears his name.

Governor Dummer was descended from the sturdiest, most influential, and most public-spirited of Puritan stock. In 1632, barely two years after John Winthrop had headed the first large group of settlers and established the Massachusetts Bay Colony at Boston, William Dummer's ancestor, Richard Dummer, and his wife Mary came to America aboard the ship *Whale* from Southampton. The spirit of adventure, as well as religious conviction, must have spurred the young people to leave England, for the Dummers were apparently well-to-do landowners at Bishopstoke, just six miles toward London from Southampton. In the wake of two hard winters in the new colony, discouraging reports were reaching England. Few were hardy enough to embark for Boston in the face of such reports. The Richard Dummers were among the 250 who, according to the records of Governor John Winthrop, were all that joined the colonists during 1632. The young couple's trip across on the *Whale* must have been an adventure, to

3

say the least, made, as it was, in the company of thirty emigrants and seventy head of cattle, all but two of which survived in good condition.

Grandfather of the founder of Governor Dummer Academy, this Richard was an energetic and influential colonist. In these respects he foreshadowed the industry and public-mindedness both of his eldest son and his famous grandsons. Just prior to emigrating to America, Richard had given into the care of his brother Stephen five acres of land in Bishopstoke, from the proceeds of which forty shillings a year were to be paid over to the parish for relief of the poor. Not this generous act alone, but a later and more striking one as well, as we shall see, gives ample evidence of a benevolent turn in mind.

Richard and Mary originally settled in the Roxbury section of Boston, where he built the first water-powered grist mill in New England. Such an enterprise was of very real value to the colonists, who otherwise must have ground their corn by hand. His family had had mill interests in England and undoubtedly Richard had learned the business there.

In 1635 Richard Dummer moved his family to the settlement of Newbury, on the banks of the Quascacunquen River (now the Parker). There he and several other men of rising influence, including Richard Saltonstall and Henry Sewall, undertook a large cattle venture which initially had apparently only indifferent success. That Mr. Dummer's prosperity as a cattle farmer increased through the years, however, is testified to by the fact that Rowley town records in 1660 contain a vote to put up "a substantial and strong three-railed fence . . . between Newbury and Rowley to prevent cattle coming from Mr. Dummer's farm," as well as the fact that, beyond his own holdings, in 1642 he was allowed to graze more than sixty head of cattle in the common pasture. Meanwhile Mr. Dummer's holdings increased until he became one of the richest men and the largest land-holders in the Colony.

A great part of his prosperity, moreover, derived from his second grist mill, at the falls of the Parker River. Originally established in 1635 (in concert with John Spencer) as a sawmill — imagine the value of sawn timber to the colonists, who had otherwise to hand-hew their own — it was apparently converted in 1638 for the grinding of corn, an equally vital service. After Spencer returned to England (as, indeed, did Mr. Dummer for a short while), in the wake of religious controversy which gathered around

Mrs. Ann Hutchinson, Richard Dummer apparently became sole owner of the business.

The upheaval which, together with the death of his wife, caused Richard's brief return to England stemmed from the strongly controversial activities of that energetic and admirable Puritan lady, Mrs. Hutchinson. Liberal for her day in her views, she believed that the individual had direct access to the grace and love of God. Such a belief was in violent opposition to the concept which was upheld by the Puritan majority, headed by Governor Winthrop, according to which the individual conscience was first of all subject to the supremacy of church and state.

Mrs. Hutchinson, mother of fourteen children even before leaving England for America, must, indeed, have possessed a compelling personality and conviction; for she drew to her support some of the most important figures of her day, including Sir Harry Vane, for a year Governor of the Colony. To her party came Mary Dummer and, apparently through her influence, her husband Richard. By this time Richard was a power in the Colony, holding the office of Assistant to the Governor.

Nevertheless, with the expulsion of Ann Hutchinson and her family to the territory of Rhode Island, her adherents suffered the displeasure of the victorious John Winthrop, now even more strongly entrenched than ever. With others Richard Dummer was dropped from the Court of Assistants and disarmed.

The great-mindedness and charity of Richard Dummer — a quality which we are to see so strongly characteristic of his grandson William — clearly displayed itself in 1640, a bare three years later. When Governor Winthrop, through the dishonesty of a retainer, suffered serious financial reverses, sympathetic colonists subscribed a fund of 500 pounds in his behalf. The largest single contributor, his donation amounting to one-fifth of the total, was Richard Dummer.

By his first wife, Mary, Richard had but one child, Shubael, a graduate of Harvard, later a minister in York, Maine, where he died in an Indian attack. In 1644 Richard took as his second wife Frances Burr, the widow of Reverend Jonathan Burr, colleague of the famous Richard Mather. She brought with her four children of her first marriage, and bore to Richard four sons and a daughter. It is in the oldest of these sons, Jeremiah, that we are primarily interested.

Apprenticed at fourteen to the highly respected and able John Hull, mint master and treasurer of the Colony, Jeremiah forged ahead quickly to become one of the most noted and admired of early American silversmiths. Highly talented artisan whose work is much admired today, engraver (he engraved plates for paper money for the Connecticut colony), possibly even a portrait painter, though this has been rigorously questioned of late, Jeremiah was an influential shipowner as well, and did not balk at outfitting privateersmen against the depredations of the French. Settling in Boston with his wife, Anna (Atwater), he played an active and important role in the affairs of the colony during the last thirty years of the seventeenth century and the first decade of the eighteenth. This energetic citizen was holder of many important positions and apparently carried out his responsibilities with high credit.

Of Jeremiah's nine children, two in particular reached positions of eminence. A son, also Jeremiah, commonly referred to as Jeremy, graduated with distinction from Harvard College. He later became a most able and intelligent agent in London for the Massachusetts and Connecticut colonies. William, as Lieutenant-Governor to the royal province of Massachusetts, performed inestimable service in a difficult and turbulent period.

The position of colonial agent in London was at best an uneasy one, for the holder had to contend both with the natural suspicion of the crown and the mistrust of his countrymen 3,000 miles away. Jeremy represented his clients well: he neither truckled under to the representatives of royalty nor hesitated to inform the colonies when he felt they were acting rashly and against their own best interests. His "A Defense of the New England Charters" in 1721, coming at a time when the question of annulling the charters was before the House of Commons, was instrumental in defeating this bill. Although he was not always appreciated back home, in spite of the contributions to the welfare of his countrymen, that Jeremy was admired in England is testified to by the following quotation, which appeared in the *London Daily Advertiser* sometime after his death.

> During a considerable part of Queen Anne's Reign he was intimate with and greatly valued by all the ministers and the brightest genius of that time, he being well skilled in the learned languages and some of the modern, thoroughly acquainted with the most valuable parts of literature, and a graceful speaker. He had a fine memory

and being of a communicative and beneficent disposition, his company was eagerly sought by all lovers of good sense and humanity.

There is one more permanent monument to Jeremy's deep interest in the welfare of Americans. While in England he, by dint of earnest and prolonged effort, succeeded in inducing Elihu Yale, who was born in America but had amassed a fortune in India, to contribute handsomely to the Collegiate School at Saybrook, Connecticut, soon to be renamed for its benefactor. Ultimately Yale's contributions to the college amounted to the largest private gift bestowed on the institution for a period of one hundred years to follow.

The sound sense and public spirit of all these Dummers, Richard, Jeremiah, and Jeremy, found itself unabated in William, the oldest surviving son of the famous silversmith. Born in 1678, he did not enter Harvard, as did his scholarly brother, but unquestionably his early education was the best to be had at the time. That William valued education highly is manifest in the very existence of this history.

Some time after his twenty-fourth birthday, it is not clear just when, William sailed for England, perhaps in connection with his father's active shipping interests. He may have remained abroad for as long as ten years. It is a matter of record that he married one of the Dummer cousins in England, settled in Plymouth, where he procured a position through the influence of his father-in-law, and remained until the death of his wife.

On May 27, 1712, he returned to America, landing at Marblehead, thirty-four years old, a widower without children. Scarcely two years later he married Catherine, the twelfth child of Thomas Dudley, who was drawing toward the end of his stormy regime as Governor of the Massachusetts colony. William appears to have had definite political ambitions, for in 1716 he visited England again just long enough to secure appointment as Lieutenant-Governor to Colonel Samuel Shute, who was being sent to succeed Dudley.

The administration of Governor Shute was, if possible, even more turbulent than that of his predecessor. After more than six years of bitter quarreling with the General Court of Massachusetts, Shute, with much of the right on his side, left for England to report his grievance to the Privy Council.

For nearly six years following, William Dummer, in his capacity as Lieutenant-Governor, assumed the duties of Governor and
Commander-in-Chief in the provincial administration. His was
the responsibility to walk a very narrow way, indeed, between the
desires of his superiors in England and the touchy tempers of the
General Court. That he was able to weather with dignity and
restraint the pressures from all sides and still govern in the best
interests of the province speaks eloquently for his qualities of mind
and heart. The administration of Governor Dummer was, relatively
speaking, a space of calm between the stormy sways of both his
predecessors and of his immediate successor.

One episode will serve to illustrate the wisdom and initiative of
William Dummer. Throughout the presence of Samuel Shute as
Governor, and before, there had been much trouble with the
Indians on the frontiers of the province, even extending back into
central Massachusetts. Any attempts at securing a permanent
peace had been but short-lived. Several efforts had been made
to induce the French Governor of Canada to join in persuading
the Indians to give over their raids, until it became clear that the
French were actually encouraging their agents to incite the
Indians to violence.

Notorious for his unrelenting hatred of the English "heretic"
was Father Sebastian Ralé, French missionary to the Norridgewock tribe in New Hampshire. (Matters became so serious that
during this period settlers could demand from the provincial
government at Boston a bounty of 100 pounds for the scalp of
an enemy savage.)

Finally atrocities at as widely separated localities as Cape
Porpoise and the Connecticut River valley around Deerfield
determined Governor Dummer to take action. By acts of compromise and moderation he won from the General Assembly
authority to act to suppress the Indians, an authority which Governor Shute had striven for but failed to accomplish.

In August, 1724, an expedition of about two hundred veteran
backwoodsmen was organized against the hotbed of Indian sav-
agery at Norridgewock. The attack by the Americans was a
bloody and spectacular success, resulting not only in the virtual
destruction of the Norridgewock strength, but also in the death of
the fiery Ralé, who refused to surrender. In August, 1726, after
having pursued the campaign grimly for two more years, Governor Dummer headed at Falmouth an imposing delegation which

concluded final terms with the sachems of the Abenake nation. The negotiations as carried on reflect highest credit upon the wisdom, justice, and strength of mind of the Governor. The terms, which were of great advantage to the white settlers, were the first to be well observed by these Indians. Twice many years later the famous Dummer treaty was to serve as the basis for arrangements of peace with the New England tribes.

Even a casual study of the administration of the province by Acting Governor Dummer gives proof of the high character of this unspectacular but able leader. In 1728 William Burnet was sent belatedly to Massachusetts as Governor Shute's successor. William Dummer retired — but not for long. Governor Burnet's tenancy lasted little over a year, a year full of bickering and ill feeling. The Lieutenant Governor again assumed the burdens of office and once more brought order to the administration. The following sentences from a letter of the famous Judge Samuel Sewall clearly imply the relief that the citizens must have felt upon the return of William Dummer to office: "These are to congratulate your honor and this province upon your returning again to be their Governor and Commander-in-Chief . . . I thank God who has reserved you against this juncture of our distress." A year later, with the appointment of a new Provincial Governor, Mr. Dummer was enabled to retire permanently and with honor from his demanding post.

William Dummer was to enjoy from this time over thirty years of retirement from political life, thirty pleasant years as a well-to-do gentleman-farmer, at the conclusion of which his days came to a peaceful close — his days, but not his contributions to his fellow man.

The nature of this venerable New Englander can be no better summed up, it seems to me, than in the words of the able historian of the Academy's first one hundred years, Nehemiah Cleaveland:

> . . . the character of William Dummer was one of uncommon symmetry. We discover no shining quality of mind — no prominent, outcropping virtue. But we do discern abilities equal to every emergency — a judgment always calm and solid — great firmness — strict integrity and warm benevolence. He may, or may not have possessed those military capabilities which, under favoring circumstances, make a hero — but in civil affairs and governmental administration he un-

doubtedly showed, to a remarkable extent, that rare combination of qualities, which, as exhibited on a broader stage, the world has since learned to admire in George Washington.

In 1712, upon his return from England, Governor Dummer had been presented by his father, Jeremiah, the "houses, lands, and farms" in Newbury, covering 330 acres, a portion of the very property which had been granted to Richard Dummer for his cattle venture nearly seventy-five years before. It is known that William and Catherine, whom he had married in 1714, were spending their summers here by 1716, when Governor Shute and his retinue, passing through to Portsmouth, enjoyed their hospitality for the night. The Mansion House was strategically located just off the Old Bay Road to the north from Boston, one of the key arteries at the time in the New England colonies. The road wound from Rowley toward the Dummer estate, approaching over a section, now discontinued, near the present school water tower and downward past Miss Degen's home. It passed the site of the milestone (dated 1708) which even today stands on the corner of the Mansion House lawn and offers the traveler the information that the distance to Boston is thirty-three miles, and to Newburyport, five. The old road continued, as today, across the hauntingly beautiful marshes and over Thurlow's (Thorla's) Bridge.

The Mansion House itself is unquestionably one of the loveliest of early New England homes. It is difficult to set a date to its original construction. One of the school's finest friends and benefactors, James Duncan Phillips, in his paper "Governor Dummer's Family and His School" favored a date sometime after the Governor's retirement in 1729. Nehemiah Cleaveland, on the other hand, supported the more traditional date, somewhere during the years 1714-1720. Whether it was to the present Mansion that Governor Shute made his visit in 1716 cannot be said for certain. The belief is, however, that William Dummer built the house as a summer home for his bride shortly after their marriage. One of the favorite legends, which abound and thrive in the venerable environment of the Byfield school, favors this belief. For it is said that when William first brought Catherine to her new home, mounted on a magnificent charger he carried her straight in the front door (which is, indeed, of such size as to lend credence to the story) and up the broad staircase to the second floor. And even to the present day, occupants of the Mansion will assure the visitor with great gravity that on warm August nights when the

The Ancient Milestone and the Mansion House

moon is full, the ghostly forms of the Governor and his lady, mounted in all their dignity on a magnificent white charger, can be seen to repeat this heroic performance.

It is this imposing estate which William Dummer, who died childless, left in the very first provision of his will for the establishment and support of a free grammar school (which in the parlance of the day meant a school of which the primary function would be instruction in the ancient and classic languages, Latin and Greek):

> I give, devise, and bequeath, unto the Rev. Mr. Thomas Foxcroft and Rev. Dr. Charles Chauncey, Ministers of the First Church in Boston aforesaid, and Mr. Nathaniel Dummer of Newbery in the county of Essex, my dwelling house and farm and all my Real Estate lying and being in Newbery . . . upon this special use and trust, viz. that the whole of Ye rents, issues and profits thereof shall in the first place be appropriated, laid out, and expended in erecting, building and finishing a Grammar school house, to be erected on the most convenient part of my farm, according to Ye appointment of the then Ministers of the parish of Byfield . . . and five of Ye principal inhabitants, free-holders of the parish . . . elected . . . for that purpose; and . . . that then Ye annual rents, issues and profits shall forever be appropriated and set apart toward the maintenance of the Grammar school Master in said school . . . and when so chosen and appointed in manner as aforesaid to be and remain Master of said school without any removal unless through sickness, advanced years and inability, or by a profligate, wicked life he shall be adjudged and sentenced by a majority of the overseers of Harvard College to be displaced . . . And it is my will that no scholar be admitted into such school but such as can read English well . . ."

It is difficult to envision a setting more lovely than that which William Dummer provided for his school. Several miles removed from the closest community, the spot remains to this day one of the most beautiful to be found on the Massachusetts shore line north of Boston. In 1761 the Governor's farmland and estate lay loosely caught between the meandering courses of the Parker and Mill Rivers as they moved toward a meeting out in the marshland at the foot of the property. The school, still occupying the area set aside for it by Governor Dummer, stands on land gently sloping upward from the flatness of the tidal marshes, looking out toward the ocean five miles to the eastward at Plum Island. Of an early morning at sunrise, the view in this direction from the master's room at the top of Peirce Hall is one which is remembered (in at least this one quarter) with pleasure akin to reverence.

The Governor had done his part. On October 26, 1761, a Boston newspaper spoke of him as follows:

> While he lived, his prayers, and his alms, continually ascended for a memorial before God. At his death, he left a great part of his estate to pious and charitable uses. Having serv'd his generation by the will of God, he fell asleep, in a joyful expectation of a resurrection to eternal life.

It remained for his friends named in the Will to follow his wishes with respect to the establishment of a school.

The Little Red Schoolhouse, restored

CHAPTER II

Master Moody

On Tuesday, March 1, 1763, sixteen months after the death of Governor Dummer, his friend the Reverend Moses Parsons of the Byfield Parish Church preached at the opening of the new Dummer School. In his daily record for that occasion one may read: "Dumr Charity School begun prayd ther in ye morng." A somewhat fuller entry, made separately, informs us that the text appropriately selected for that event was from Isaiah 32:8— "But the liberal deviseth liberal things, and by liberal things shall he stand." Now, two hundred years later, Governor Dummer Academy still stands and flourishes, a memorial to the liberal thoughts and acts of her founder and a tribute to the determination of other liberal-minded men to nurture and increase what the Governor had planted.

The three Trustees named in the Will had seen to it that income from the rental of the Mansion House and farm during 1762 was used to provide for the building of the first schoolhouse. The parish committee, of which Moses Parsons was an influential (if not the leading) member, had designated a site in front of the Mansion House, a little toward Newburyport. The modest, one-story building that was erected there contained but two rooms, and a vestibule with facilities for hanging jackets and coats, the whole of this covering an area of but twenty by thirty feet. The Little Red Schoolhouse (and that it was actually red in color is confirmed in a letter of Nehemiah Cleaveland, who studied there under Isaac Smith very early in the nineteenth century) stands to this day in a prominent spot on the Academy campus. It has survived a checkered career and many moves. Finally, in 1938, it was beautifully and authentically restored, even to the inside furnishings. Some of these furnishings — the wide wooden armchair, the pair of scales, the stem-winding watch — are those actually used by the redoubtable Master Moody. Appropriately a British union jack hangs from the flag standard, for Governor Dummer's school pre-dates our nation.

All was not easy. At the very beginning there was agitation amongst the parishioners of Byfield for arranging that the school be set up nearer to the center of the parish. The provisions of the

13

Governor's will, however, were specific, and the parish committee and Trustees stuck to their guns. The schoolhouse was placed "on the most convenient part" of the farm, which was located in the northeast corner of the parish.

A year after the school had been opened, the Newbury representative to the General Court of the Province was instructed by the parish to ask clarification of the following questions concerning the Dummer estate:

1. Who are the Persons that are to Rent sd farm, to repair the Buildings, to Receive the Rents, and to pay the same to the Master of the school?

2. What number of those persons mentioned in the sd Governor Dummer's will (to direct and appoint in the affair of the Master And said school) are to be agreed, so as to make a Valid act?

3. Who is to Judg or Say when Scholars are qualified for sd School, according to the Will of the Doner, and what other Larning besides grammar, that first Being Duly Regarded, is to be taught In sd School?

4. Who are the Persons that are to have the Care and Inspection of sd Master and School?

In the words of Nehemiah Cleaveland, "This literal transcript from the Records, indicates, at least, that the school was not founded too soon"! The questions are purely academic, however. Indeed, there is no evidence that any official action was taken on them. For, once the committees had done their parts in setting up the buildings and procuring Samuel Moody as the first Master, they had little more to do than to sit back and admire their handiwork — as well they might. For Master Moody made the first three decades of the Dummer School years of unsurpassed accomplishment and set up a challenge not only for those who were to follow him in this school, but in all private preparatory schools everywhere — a challenge in the form of a standard of performance which has perhaps been matched by a few, but exceeded by none.

One cannot read an account of Sam Moody without being caught up by the compelling power of the man's personality. Most of the well known "facts" about him come to us second-hand at best. The man is in large part a legendary figure, yet each anecdote which goes to create this legend fits so comfortably with every other as to give considerable assurance that the popular concept of Master Moody cannot be far from accurate.

It is clear without question that the first schoolmaster at Dummer was held in the utmost respect and affection by practically all the boys who studied under him. That he was an able tutor was not to be questioned. Equally without question his habits and his methods were eccentric, as we shall see. Surest of all, however, is the fact that here was a remarkably talented teacher of youth, in the fullest sense of that phrase. Completely dedicated, single-mindedly enthusiastic, quick and severe in criticizing, but ready with praise when it was deserved — a man who set, and lived by, high standards — Samuel Moody was a teacher rarely gifted. Whenever this is true, today as two hundred years ago, method matters little.

Master Moody came honestly by the oddities of his nature. His grandfather was the eminent Samuel "Father" Moody of York (now in Maine — then part of Massachusetts), of whom it is said: "He was a man of remarkable piety and was greatly beloved and no less feared by the people of his charge . . ." A graduate of Harvard in 1697, minister of the First Parish Church of York for almost fifty years (where he, coincidentally, succeeded the ill-fated Shubael Dummer), he was a clergyman widely known in his day, famed equally for this "uncommon benevolence" and his eccentricity. Both are amply demonstrated in the following episode, described in the delightful little volume *Biographical Sketches of the Moody Family:*

> It is related, that on a cold, frosty morning, a poor woman came into his house without any shoes on her feet. Learning, on inquiry, that she was destitute of those necessary articles, he went to the bedside and took his wife's only pair of shoes and gave them to the poor woman. When his wife arose she made diligent search for her shoes, but on Father Moody's coming into the room he told her he had given them away to a poor woman. "Dear Mr. Moody," she said, "how could you do so, when you know they were all the shoes I had in the world?" He replied, "Oh never mind it, dear wife, the Lord will send another pair before night, I doubt not." In the course of the forenoon a neighbor brought in a pair of new shoes, stating that they were too small for his wife, and he thought he would bring

them over to give to Mrs. Moody, if she would like them!

It is a sore temptation to revel in the luxuriant crop of anecdote, apocryphal or not, which has grown up around "Father" Moody, for it is from such that an insight into the human qualities of the man seems to grow. The same is, indeed, the case with his famous grandson, our Master Moody; from the vigor of the Moody stock legend grew and thrived. Surely much that is told in it is true of the men, if not of their lives. Suffice it to say of Father Samuel, however, that in him there were in abundance that vitality of mind and body, that faith, courage, and resolution, and those oddities of behavior which loomed large in the character of his grandson.

Nor was Joseph, the father of Master Moody, lacking in the qualities which seem both the strength and the weakness of the strain. The eccentric character of "Handkerchief" Moody, so-called from the silk handkerchief which during the whole latter half of his life he wore over his face when in public, has been somewhat mystically depicted in Nathaniel Hawthorne's short romance "The Minister's Black Veil." Several explanations are given for Joseph's odd behavior, the most current being that he veiled his face as the result of his having accidentally been the cause of the death of a young friend during his boyhood, an incident which evidently preyed on his mind ever after. Despite his strange affliction and the peculiar behavior derived from it, Joseph Moody was known as a kindly and pious man, and throughout his life was particularly famed for his eloquent prayers. Like his father and his son a graduate of Harvard College, he was at first very active in the civic affairs of York, Maine, achieving the office of Judge of the County Court. Then for six years he was active in the ministry, before his aberration caused his virtual retirement.

When Master Moody arrived in Byfield to take over the "Dumr Charity School," he was already a teacher of long experience, and widely known. In 1746 he had graduated from Harvard. He was ranked fifth in his class at graduation, the order of the graduates being established at that time (to quote the Quinquennial Catalogue) "according to the precedence of their parents." While at college, after waiting on table during his first two years, he succeeded in earning scholarships.

Indications are that upon graduation from Harvard the young man preached on occasion, supplying pulpits in the neighborhood of his York home in the Province of Maine. Apparently he was at one time invited to settle in a parish living — but only in the case that another, to whom the living was to be offered first, should fail to accept. Whether the terms of this offer served as a dampener upon Master Moody's aspirations as a preacher or, more likely, whether he simply concluded from his experience that his talents and tastes did not lie in that direction — whatever the case, to the great good fortune of all concerned Samuel turned to school-teaching. In all likelihood he began not long after leaving college. At first he taught in the public grammar school at York. Later, in 1756, he started a school of his own in the same town. There he was able to place the academic emphasis upon the study of the learned languages Latin and Greek, wherein lay his consuming interest.

That students came from far as well as near to study under Moody is evident from two brief examples. From Biddeford, twenty-five miles to the north of York, came Joseph Willard. Willard's means were very limited, but when the young man considered abandoning his pursuit of an education, Master Moody pronounced in his abrupt and loud schoolmaster style, "Willard you must go to college"! Sidney Willard in his memoirs continues this description of his father's propulsion into further education:

> Though the words of the master might seem too impulsive, their sincerity was soon demonstrated. By his generous efforts a subscription for Willard's board was immediately procured; his master charged him nothing for tuition, offered him as a candidate for Harvard College, in about a year, and by his disinterested services in behalf of his meritorious pupil contributed largely to the success of his application to become a beneficiary scholar.

If Samuel Moody had at that time been told that his young pupil would later become, for the period of almost a quarter of a century, one of Harvard's most respected presidents, it would have been characteristic of him to evince loud enthusiasm — and not the slightest degree of surprise.

To Master Moody, all the way from Northampton, Massachusetts, came another boy destined for greatness: Caleb Strong, for a total of eleven years during the first two decades of the nineteenth century Governor of the Commonwealth of Massachusetts. Sober, strong-hearted, and even-tempered, this able man was to guide the fortunes of his state through some of its most critical years, particularly during the War of 1812. Such men as Willard and Strong did Master Moody's reputation draw to his schools.

Tradition has it that Master Moody's obvious qualifications for the seat at Governor Dummer's new school were brought to the attention of Moses Parsons and his committee of Byfield freeholders by none other than the famous British evangelist, the "Great Awakener" George Whitefield. Mr. Whitefield had been well acquainted with Master Moody's grandfather. (A delightful story is told of Grandfather Samuel when Whitefield landed in York in 1744. "Sir," said the old man, "you are, first, welcome to America; secondly, to New England; thirdly, to all faithful ministers in New England; fourthly, to all the good people of New England; fifthly, to all the good people of York; and sixthly and lastly, to me, dear sir, less than the least of all." Master Moody's celebrated gift for rhetoric was honestly come by!)

However the news of this able and energetic teacher's talents reached Byfield, certain it is that he was, without loss of time, prevailed upon to come there to take charge of the new institution. For very shortly after the school house had been constructed, on February 28 in 1763, the following entry appeared in the diary of the Reverend Mr. Parsons: "Dummer Charity School opened Feb. 28 pd [preached] upn ye occasion a public lecture fr'm Isai 32:8. When Mr. Sam Moody of York took charge thereof. . ." School began the next day.

Since there are no Trustees' records covering the first twenty years of the school's existence, no complete record exists of the circumstances under which Master Moody assumed direction of the new Grammar School, the first of its kind in the country. By provision of the Will of William Dummer, the Master was to hold his position for life unless because of sickness, age, ineptitude, or profligacy he were to be disqualified by the Board of Overseers of Harvard College. After the school house had been built, all "annual rents, issues and profits" of the estate were to be appropriated to his use at the school. He had the Governor's Mansion as a dwelling place and as a boarding house for as many boys as could be accommodated; he had the farm, from which could be drawn many of the supplies to fill the needs of his little community. In addition, as superintendent of this farm, as well as of the boarding aspects of the school and the general administrative detail, Master Moody brought with him his brother Joseph, whose practical mind and administrative talent relieved the preceptor of all of the burden except that directly related to the discipline of the students and the pursuit of learning. What more ideal situation could have greeted a talented and ambitious schoolmaster?

And what more remarkably talented schoolmaster than Samuel Moody? The field was his and his alone for almost two decades. Surely there can be no better evidence of the great man's skill as a teacher and leader of boys than the achievement made by these same boys in later life. 526 of them came to Dummer to Master Moody. Score upon score of them emerged in later years at the forefront of a multitude of fields of occupation: as theologians, teachers, and scholars; members of Congress for the new United States (eleven served in the House of Representatives, five in the Senate); lawyers; physicians; merchants; government officials; military leaders; diplomats; judges; members of state legislatures; philanthropists; as well as shipowners and shipmasters; privateersmen; surveyors; artists; clockmakers; and as those leaders in local affairs, the moderators of town meetings. Some of these have already been identified. The entire list comprises an awesome monument to the man who gave these men their early training. (One brief vital statistic, from which can be inferred something of the quality of Master Moody's school: It was customary for candidates for higher education to enter college at the age of fourteen. One youngster, Samuel Cooper Johonnot, who came under the energetic supervision of Samuel Moody at the age of seven, entered Harvard just short of his twelfth birthday. He was later appointed American Consul in the West Indies.)

Anecdotes of varying degrees of authenticity compound to offer a life-like portrait of this most interesting and admirable pedagogue. Some, like those passed down by Nehemiah Cleaveland and Sidney Willard, are the testimonies of men who knew well many of Master Moody's students and closest friends. (Indeed, Sidney Willard himself remembered Moody clearly from frequent visits that the old man had made to President Willard's home.) Other stories may have less direct sources; but all tend to the same effect.

The consensus reveals Samuel Moody not as a scholar of encyclopaedic knowledge, but rather as a practical-minded instructor thoroughly versed in his Latin and Greek texts — which he demanded that his students con with the greatest care and accuracy. That he was neither highly skilled nor much interested in the fields of mathematics and natural science seems clear. Yet, though the learned languages comprised the main body of the curriculum, the sciences were by no means ignored. Older boys and, at intervals, paid assistants were entrusted with instruction in these subjects. When in 1786, due to the indisposition of Master Moody, the Trustees (under the recent Act of Incorporation) appealed to Harvard for a "learned and prudent assistant," Samuel Webber, a former Dummer boy and, as we have seen, later to become President of Harvard, was supplied to fill in (at the salary, incidentally, of ten pounds monthly). Mathematics and science could hardly have suffered from this arrangement, for in 1789 Mr. Webber was to become Professor of Mathematics and Natural Philosophy at the College.

Nehemiah Cleaveland relates that the Master carried on continual close perusal of both the Latin and French dictionaries from "A" to "Z", evidence of his concern for exactness of knowledge. Whereas, however, a French instructor was from time to time hired to instruct the boys in that tongue (it may be doubted whether Samuel Moody's Yankee twang was well adapted to pronunciation of French vowels), it was not so with the ancient languages. Here the great man was in his element. Cleaveland tells how when Theophilus Parsons was presiding at the Bench he would on occasion lean forward, whisper to the Court Reporter, another Dummer boy, and pronounce the following judgment upon the learning of a lawyer appearing before him: "This brother of ours did not learn his Latin under Master Moody."

Master Moody was first and foremost a teacher gifted with a rare knowledge of his subject, and a way with his students.

> He had, to begin with, certain qualities of intellect, heart, and temperament, which made it comparatively easy for him either to curb or to stimulate the youthful mind . . . During his first twenty years as Master of Dummer School, he *was* MASTER to all intents and purposes . . . He had the good sense to see that in the earlier stages of education — if not, indeed, in every stage — manner and quality are definitely more important than variety and quantity.

We may see reflected in this account some of the estimable Nehemiah's own outlook on education, but there shines through, as well, a clear insight into Samuel Moody's gift with boys. "He knows the way to touch their hearts," quotes Cleaveland.

It is not hard to picture that honest, forthright first Master at

Dummer School, vigorous and sometimes boisterous, solidly settled back in his capacious armchair, robed in a great, loose, wide-sleeved gown, with a tasseled cap askew on his head (for so one of his pupils recalled him years later). From time to time he would consult the old stem-winder on the desk before him, meanwhile continually exhorting his boys to fruitful labor. His whole mind was concentrated on the progress of his lads, with an energy, earnestness, and enthusiasm which were at the same time impressive and infectious. Nor was his sole concern with the intellectual development of his pupils. Himself an inveterate horseback rider and an ardent swimmer, in seasonable weather and when the tide was right, his powerful voice would penetrate the confused hum of the classroom with the pronouncement that all should immediately depart for the swimming holes, the older boys to the banks of the Parker, the younger to a shallower stream nearby. What storm of splashing and spirited horseplay ensued can easily be imagined.

One is reluctant to pass over anecdotes relating to Master Moody's preceptorship. Several are detailed in Nehemiah Cleaveland's *Centennial Discourse:* such, for example, as the tale of the introduction of dancing to the curriculum (a horrifying development, in the eyes of the strict Calvinists of the day), and under a French dancing master, at that. Needless to say, the violent opposition of Deacon Benjamin Colman and other of the more conservative inhabitants of Byfield deterred the doughty Samuel not at all. The legends are legion, but unhappily there is not space in which to tell them all.

Master Moody firmly believed that silence was a greater deterrent to productive study in the classroom than sound (an interesting thesis, and not without considerable merit), and so each boy was encouraged to review his lessons out loud. Yet do not conclude that the resultant hubbub served to cloak unscholarly behavior. The Master's eyes and ears were attuned to the slightest discord as evidence of shirking. Woe betide the poor scholar so ill-advised as to risk the consequences of such lax behavior!

Many and various are the versions of young Edward Preble's encounter with Mr. Moody's impulsive nature — and with the honest teacher's staunch appreciation of merit, which customarily seasoned his anger and, consequently, retained the respect of his charges. It appears most likely that the sturdy Preble, later to become the scourge of the Barbary pirates, had too forcefully and somewhat bloodily punished an erring fellow student during a recess. His ire aroused, Master Moody loudly admonished the recreant, who apparently remained unrepentant. Seizing the fire shovel, for his temper was mercurial, the Schoolmaster rushed the boy, swinging the implement violently against the desktop, narrowly missing the head of the object of his displeasure. The older and the younger man — the latter upright and unmoved — locked glances for a moment.

"Boys," said the Master, returning to his seat, his anger at once evaporated, "did you observe the Brigadier when I struck? (Preble's father was, indeed, a Brigadier.) He never winked. He'll be a general yet." And in his prediction Master Moody was very close to being right.

Such was the famous Master Moody of Dummer Academy. At the height of his powers, his idiosyncrasies served merely to confirm his genius as a teacher of boys. Outgoing, domineering, vital, he devoted himself entirely to his responsibilities. Quick-tempered and impatient, but sympathetic all the same, his concern was ever for his boys; and if he drove them hard, he also drove himself. He understood boys, and they respected and admired him.

Yet the time arrived when it became increasingly clear that the Dummer School's greatest asset, this single-minded devotion of Samuel Moody, might eventually prove to be her undoing. As he grew older the Preceptor became more and more subject to the extremes of humor which had plagued his antecedents: full of vitality and radiating good spirits at one occasion, he might fall into a fit of depression at another. It was probably a prevision of what might come to be (rather than any overt episode) which prompted those interested in the school to persuade the Reverend Dr. Chauncey, sole remaining representative of the three Trustees named in the Governor's Will, to petition the legislature for an Act of Incorporation, a move which would put the institution under direct supervision of a Board of Trustees entrusted with clear powers and responsibilities.

This Act was passed in the year 1782 and specifically named to the new Board fifteen men, including Dr. Chauncey, Moses Parsons, Joseph Willard, and Samuel Moody himself. It is clear from the records that this body did not immediately find it necessary to take measures concerning the academic affairs of the school. Even as late as 1786, when Master Moody's failing health necessitated the appeal to Harvard for an assistant, the Board's concern seemed more with the management of the farm and the maintenance of the property than with the instruction of the boys.

Nevertheless, Master Moody was becoming more and more unpredictable. His customary energy occasionally bordered on coarseness, and his volubility on garrulousness. Even allowing for the frequently sarcastic judgment of that eminent man John Quincy Adams, then just a law apprentice in the Newburyport office of Theophilus Parsons, references to Master Moody in his 1787-88 diary clearly reflect the change. Having described the old man in one place as possessing "the address . . . very much that of a schoolmaster, whose habits of commanding give him a prescriptive title to importance," he indulges in greater detail in another:

> Mr. Moody was extremely full of high flown compliments; the grossest, and most fulsome flattery was incessantly in his mouth. Every virtue and every accomplishment he lavished away upon the company with so little consideration that he seemed to forget that modesty was in the list.

This loss of a sense of proportion in the good-hearted old pedagogue is likewise reflected in the extravagant language of his long letter to Joseph Willard in 1787, recommending his former student and his assistant, Samuel Webber, for consideration for a post on the Harvard faculty. Yet that Master Moody had not lost his sense of humor is evidenced by the note he jotted at the head of this same letter before sending it off: "That you may not be run down & quite out of breath, I must pray dear Sir that you would peruse this formidable Length of Letter in 4 divisions and at 4 sessions.") Certainly the old man had fallen from the height of those powers the memory of which remained green in the minds of so many of his famous graduates. Joseph Hale Abbot, a student at Dummer in the second decade of the nineteenth century passed on the following anecdote which tradition had handed down to the boys of his day:

> Master Moody, whose intellect was somewhat disordered in his old age was invited . . . to hear a distinguished advocate address the jury in an important case then pending. On leaving the courthouse, Master Moody, being asked what he thought of the orator, replied: "He is a great orator; but he would be a much greater one if he would pluck some of the feathers from the wings of his imagination and put them into the tail of his judgment."

The tail being, of course, the rudder of the bird! Even in his old age Samuel Moody, if his sense of proportion was awry, had lost none of his native perspicacity.

On the seventh of October, 1789, Master Moody conveyed to the Trustees a provisional resignation, dependent upon their granting to Joseph Moody an extension of one year on the lease of the estate. Seven weeks later the Trustees replied, expressing their inclination to accept the Preceptor's resignation according to his suggestion, "unless you shall be made sensible that it will be to your advantage to resign sooner." The records reflect an urgent desire to persuade Mr. Moody, whom the Trustees felt to be seriously impaired in his faculties, to sever his connection with the school before he should lose the reputation "so largely enjoyed" and expose himself "to the public odium." It is bluntly pointed out in their letter that rumors were rife to the effect that the Master was applying the funds of the estate to his own purposes. They were eager to avoid any kind of embarrassment. Happily no further issue seems to have been made of this circumstance; and later, in their expression of appreciation for the retiring preceptor's service to the school, the Trustees express "their due Sense and Appreciation of . . . his Distinguished Attention to the Wellfare of the Academy and his unremitted Exertions to promote it."

The final resignation came on December 16, and in it was no restriction involving the retention of Joseph as manager of the estate:

Newbury, December 16th 1789

Gentlemen:

At your last annual meeting on the first Wednesday of October last, you will remember that in my proposal then made to you of resigning my Office of Preceptor of the Academy whereof you are Trustees at the time mentioned, I reserved liberty of making my Resignation Sooner if I should think proper. Agreeable to that Reservation, and in Consideration of my increasing Indisposition and ill health, I now beg leave to inform you that I have concluded to resign my Said Office on the twenty fifth Day of March next, and do hereby desire and Request that my Resignation thereof may take place on that Day.

I am Gentlemen your very humble Servant

Samuel Moody

The resignation was accepted at the next meeting, on December 30, 1789, and a graceful expression of "regret, condolence, congratulation and good wishes" (Nehemiah Cleaveland's terms) was inscribed in the records — a copy to be sent to Mr. Moody.

How, then, at the beginning of the year 1790 stood the condition and reputation of the Academy? Certainly its years of prosperity and renown under Master Moody were but slightly dimmed by recent circumstances. The greatest change prior to the momentous resignation had come with the Act of Incorporation, passed by the legislature of the Commonwealth on October 3, 1782. The purpose of the Act, as stated in the Preamble, was to enable the carrying out of "the views of the Donor" by "erecting a Body Politic and Corporate, and investing it with certain necessary powers which could not be effected by him in his Last Will and Testament. . . ." The Board was named in the Act and its powers specified. Prominent among these were the power to elect "such Preceptors, Masters, and ushers of the said Academy as they shall judge best; and to determine the Duties and Tenures of the several Offices"; to establish "reasonable rules", with "reasonable penalties for the good Government of Said Academy"; and to supervise the admission of students. The management of the Estate was placed in their care, for disposition as they saw fit. Precaution was taken at the time to provide that the school remain where it was and that Samuel Moody continue as Preceptor, " . . . removable in the same manner and for the same Causes and by the same Authority" as specified in the original Will.

One other careful provision was made: that should the money of the Estate cease to be applied to the purpose of the school for a space of two years, then the Estate as described in the Will would revert to the Dummer heirs, and that any additional estate that might have come under the supervision of the Trust in the meantime enure to the benefit of the Corporation of Harvard College. Unquestionably these provisos have in the years since 1782, at those times when the fortunes of the Academy have reached a low ebb, been instrumental in motivating special efforts to revitalize the institution.

From this time a careful record of the affairs of the Academy, insofar as they have concerned the Trustees, has been maintained. An interesting aspect of these records is the fact that for the first six and one half years they are copied in the handsome and meticulous hand of John Quincy Adams, sixth President of the United

States, then a student in the office of Theophilus Parsons (whose father was a member of the Trust).

One additional important change was to greet the successor to Samuel Moody. Upon accepting the resignation of the first Preceptor, the Board's very next act was to decree the incompatibility of the offices of Preceptor and member of the Trust. It was voted that thereafter no preceptor be permitted to hold membership on the Board. In his Appendix to the *Centennial Discourse,* Nehemiah Cleaveland vehemently expressed his disapproval of this provision, citing the fact that at most other successful schools and colleges one position implied the other. The fact remains that no preceptor of Dummer Academy for over 100 years after Samuel Moody was to be a member of the Board.

Master Moody retained his trusteeship long enough to see Isaac Smith elected as his successor at the head of the Academy; he was, in fact, present at the meeting where the choice was made. Shortly thereafter he proffered his resignation, informing the other members that "his Situation and circumstances were such that he could no longer be likely to promote the interest of Dummer Academy as a Trustee . . . "

For the remaining five years of his life, he traveled widely, a welcome visitor at the homes of his multitude of friends and former students. Sidney Willard's accounts of Master Moody's visits to his father's home are full of affection and admiration for the old man. In the words of Cleaveland:

> He was yet strong in body, and rode much on horseback around the country . . . his large heart still beating with benevolent impulse, and his over-active brain full of grand, impracticable schemes for the advancement of education and the benefit of mankind.

One would like to credit the legend that has the doughty Samuel encounter his death, while striding energetically up and down his room, earnestly discoursing in Latin. The facts, however, are not in accord with this tradition. Master Moody in fact died on December 18, 1795, at the home of a former pupil, Dr. Samuel Tenney of Exeter, New Hampshire. The diary of Jonathan Sayward quotes from a letter which the writer had received from Dr. Tenney:

> . . . he came by my House about sunset in good spirits but informed me that he had Had a severe conflict with

the Elements, the late severe storm and was seriously overcome. he drank a Cup of tea and Complained of being sick at his stomack. Proposed a walk to Judge Parsons, appeared to be weak and Easing, but still in good Spirits his sickness at his Stomach Continuing he Got up and after walking forward to move across the room, fell suddenly and expired in about five minutes — without Discovering any perception of his Situation.

A former student at York, the Reverend Mr. Tompson of Berwick, preached the funeral sermon, which is an unusual one for the day. Instead of being solely a moral lecture couched in general terms, it treats Samuel Moody considerably in detail, building an admirable picture of the good and great-minded teacher. The burial, too, was in York, in the cemetery opposite the Meeting House. There on the gravestone, under "two of the happiest and most cherubic stone faces north of Boston," one may find the following inscription:

Integer vitae scelerisque purus

SAMUEL MOODY, Esq.

PRECEPTOR OF DUMMER ACADEMY

The first Institution of the kind in Massachusetts

He left no child to mourn his sudden death,

(for he died a bachelor,)

Yet his numerous pupils in the United States will ever

retain a lively sense of the sociability, industry,

integrity, and piety, he possessed in an un-

common degree; as well as the disinter-

ested, zealous, faithful and useful

manner he discharged the

duties of the Academy

for thirty years.

He died at Exeter, Dec. 14 [sic] 1795

aged seventy.

CHAPTER III

Isaac Smith

An entry for June 26, 1790, in the valuable journal of Salem's indefatigable diarist William Bentley reports the following: "It has been said that Dummer Academy in Newbury has been offered to Revd Mr. Isaac Smith, the present Librarian at Cambridge and that he has been down to review it. The present annual rent of the farm is 80 pounds." In actuality Mr. Smith had been chosen for the post as early as the preceding April, according to the minutes of a Trustees' meeting during that month. At this meeting compensation had been set at "rents, issues, and profits of the estate. . .deducting therefrom sufficient for the necessary reparation of the estate . . . " In addition, permission was given to charge tuition at the rate of twenty-eight shillings per pupil (an assessment shortly afterward changed to one shilling per week).

By request of the new Preceptor, the school was suspended for a period of about thirteen months following the departure of Master Moody. The thirteen month interim was put to good use by the Trustees, who took the opportunity to make extensive repairs on the Mansion House and the Schoolhouse (as well they might, considering the effect that over two decades of occupancy by hordes of boys must inevitably have wrought). Cost of the improvements amounted to approximately 100 pounds or, according to Bentley's estimate, more than the annual income from the estate.

On April 25, 1791, sessions began again, marking the start of a period of leadership at the school exceeded in length by that of only four men in its 200 year history. Scholarly and benevolent as he unquestionably was, however, Isaac Smith unfortunately lacked that commanding quality of personality which had enabled Master Moody to supervise crowds of energetic youths with deceptive ease. Nehemiah Cleaveland, who studied at the Academy briefly just a year before the new Preceptor's resignation in 1809, reports that the student body at that time amounted to slightly less than a dozen boys. The reasons for the decline at the school we shall see.

Isaac Smith, son of a Boston merchant, graduated from Harvard in 1767, having prepared for the ministry. Before returning to

Harvard in the capacity of tutor in 1774-75, he had traveled extensively in Europe and in England. There is ample evidence that throughout his life he retained an eager interest in learning and a passion for reading. He was a man of wide information and understanding, an interesting and instructive companion. Whether because during his first trip to England he had already engaged to accept the pastorate of a small dissenting congregation near Exeter (as certain of his fervently loyal former students years later insisted in letters to Nehemiah Cleaveland), or whether as Cleaveland surmised he shared Tory sentiments with many estimable countrymen, he removed to Great Britain barely a month after the Battle of Lexington and assumed the pulpit of a small church at Sidmouth. Records such as the diary of his good friend and countryman Samuel Curwen make it clear that Mr. Smith endeared himself to his congregation, and it must have been with much regret that they released him in 1784 and saw him leave again for America.

In 1787 Mr. Smith became Librarian at his alma mater in Cambridge, a position which he still held when appointed by the Trustees of Dummer Academy. In this important capacity he supervised the compiling of the first complete catalogue of the Harvard College Library.

It is very likely that for some years under Preceptor Smith the Academy enjoyed continued prosperity. He assumed control of the school while its reputation was still strong; many of Master Moody's own students quite naturally entered their own sons in their old school. The new master's qualifications as a teacher were beyond question. President Woods of Bowdoin College wrote in his sketch of Professor Parker Cleaveland, a Byfield boy and a graduate of Dummer: "The Preceptor of the Academy at this time was the Rev. Isaac Smith, who though esteemed inferior to his immediate predecessor, the renowned and eccentric Master Moody, as a disciplinarian and teacher of Latin and Greek, was regarded as much his superior in general scholarship and polite culture . . ." All reports point to him as a learned and delightful person.

True it is, too, that from his classes came numbers of able and valuable citizens. Professor Cleaveland, the young nation's first celebrated mineralogist and geologist, and the redoubtable Nehemiah were but two. Likewise students under the amiable Mr. Smith were the three brothers of the remarkable Jackson family of Newburyport. Charles, the oldest, from a Justice of the

Supreme Judicial Court of Massachusetts became a foremost and active authority in the fields of American government and law. James, an outstanding doctor and professor of medicine at Harvard Medical School, was a leading figure in the establishment of the great Massachusetts General Hospital in Boston. Patrick, at first an astute sea captain and merchant, was the prime mover in the founding of the city of Lowell and the development of the cotton industry there. All three boys attended Dummer Academy early in Isaac Smith's tenure.

History is indebted to Nehemiah Cleaveland for an attractive and sympathetic portraiture of his former tutor, and in it appears clear indication of the source of the old man's difficulties:

> In every considerable number of pupils there will be some who are not only willing, but desirous and determined to make the most of their time and opportunities. Such boys found in Isaac Smith a pleasant and profitable teacher. Not so with the idle, the roguish, and the vicious. These abused his easy good nature — shirked their duties — and played all manner of tricks on the kind-hearted, unsuspecting old man. From persons who witnessed or perhaps even abetted those pleasing performances, I have heard stories which made me laugh I confess:—but never — let me say this in extenuation of my offense — never without an indignant regret that the young rascals generally escaped the drubbing they so richly deserved.

> In the latter years of Mr. Smith's stay here, the attendance was variable and small . . . One of my studies was Virgil. At stated times the whole class, consisting of one pupil, went up for recitation to the Preceptor's desk. There he sat in his soft-cushioned, square-seated, round-backed arm chair, a short, nice, rubicund, but kindly and scholarly looking old gentleman. As the recitation proceeded, you may well suppose that it was very gratifying to me to see how much confidence he had in his pupil. Gradually his large round eyes would close — his head would droop — and there would be every outward indication that he was taking a comfortable nap. Now and then, however, if the translation was not very bad, he would murmur a sleepy assent. And in fact I had reason to think that he followed me all along — for whenever I made an egregious blunder, it woke him instantly.

His good humor was sometimes pleasantly displayed under circumstances that might have embarrassed other men. At one time, when his school had nearly reached the vanishing point, some person in a neighboring town innocently asked him how many pupils he had. Mr. Smith at once assumed a puzzled expression of face, as if engaged in a computation of some difficulty, and then with a doubtful twist of the mouth and a prolonged utterance of the definite and conjectural adjective, replied — "I have s-o-m-e ONE." . . .

Mr. Smith returned to Boston where he served for many years as Chaplain of the Alms House. His declining days were made comfortable and happy by the kindness of friends and relatives, and for twenty years longer he lived on — a man of singular purity, gentleness and piety — venerated and beloved by all who knew him.

Mr. Smith's strength obviously did not lie in the direction of discipline. This weakness was aggravated by the fact that during his preceptorship, at a time when the ports of Salem and Newburyport were busily engaged in trade with the French West Indies, the Academy became the seat of education for a number of boys from Guadeloupe and Martinique, almost forty being on record as having attended the school during this period. Many of these young gentlemen ("animal exotics from the torrid zone" is Nehemiah Cleaveland's phrase) were neither distinguished nor ambitious as scholars and were apparently a source of sore perplexity to the good Mr. Smith.

Yet many boys had reason to remember the old man with affection. Indeed, in 1802 one Joseph Grafton wrote his mother from the school that "Mr. Smith and I play backgammon he is very fond of it" and later assured her, "You need not be worried about my being fit for College next year for I expect to be perfectly as well fitted as the Andover boys, if not better." But the school did not thrive. One report has it that the Master conducted the daily prayers with his eyes open to prevent boys from deviltry. Finally, in June of 1807, the Trustees began to show concern over "the present declining state of the Academy."

At this time, a quarter of a century after the original Act of Incorporation, only two of the fifteen men originally appointed by the Commonwealth were still on the Board: Dr. Micajah Sawyer, eminent Newburyport physician and the Board's Treasurer;

and the Reverend Thomas Cary, who served a total of twenty-six years, although paralyzed during a good part of his term. The President was Judge Ebenezer March, who for twelve more years was to give the Academy valuable service. Other prominent and influential citizens were among the members: Chief Justice Theophilus Parsons, who was at the same time a Fellow of Harvard College; and John Snelling Popkin, a professor at Harvard, preacher, and humorist of note. Several of the Trustees were former students of Master Moody and had known the school almost from its inception: among them, William Coombs, Enoch Sawyer, Benjamin Colman, and Deacon Joseph Hale (notorious with the boys for his severity and sharp temper, which he invoked as major domo of his boarding house near the Academy), in addition to Justice Parsons. Elijah Parish, Nathaniel Carter, Edward Little, and Ebenezer Parsons completed the group in 1807 — but for one more. Recording the acts of the Board at this juncture in the school's history was a man who was completing the first third of his forty-nine years of service on the Board, a man for whose painstaking penmanship any reader of the minutes is deeply grateful, the Reverend John Andrews of Newburyport.

This august body chose from its membership President March, Edward Little and William Coombs to initiate an inquiry, consult with Preceptor Smith, and ". . . report what measures in their opinion should be pursued to promote the usefulness of the Academy." From the reports it is clear that the Trustees were concerned especially about the sharp decrease in enrollment. Bentley in his journal for March 21, 1793, had reported only "about twenty youth at the Academy." There is, however, reference to the presence of an Assistant Preceptor, perhaps as late as 1804, which would suggest that the enrollment at that time could not have dropped much since 1793 and may have risen, yet two years later the following entry appears in the minutes:

> Voted that when the number of scholars in the Academy shall amount to 25, that the Preceptor be authorized to employ if he shall think fit an assistant . . .

No assistant appears on the record during Isaac Smith's time after this entry (or for two years before). This tell-tale provision, joined to Nehemiah Cleaveland's testimony to an enrollment of "not quite a dozen" in 1809 would seem to be mute, but conclusive evidence that the school was losing patronage rapidly.

The committee's report two months after its appointment aims a gentle, but firm remonstrance at Society at large for the "too general fondness in mankind for new institutions," while deploring the "multiplying of Academies" and the "specious proclamations of the advantage to be obtained at them."

It goes on to state:

> . . . Another cause for the decline of Dummer Academy is a report which has been too extensively circulated that the Preceptor has been too indulgent to his pupils and has suffered them to disregard his own rules with impunity.
>
> It has also been said that such accommodations as to board, and attention to manners and propriety of conduct, in a family which Parents wish for their children is not to be obtained at so reasonable a price as at other Academies. — Now whether these reports are true or not, whether they are circulated by persons interested in other Academies, or by persons inattentive to the consequences of such reports, the effect is the same, and the great question is, how shall the Trustees remedy or counteract the evils? —
>
> Your committee feeling great respect for our Preceptor, as a man of learning, of benevolence and piety and not doubting but that he will exert himself in the performance of his whole duty; — propose to the Trustees the following measures. —
>
> 1. That no scholar be admitted only he engages to tarry and conform to the rules and orders of the Academy for a time equal to one term in the Academy, — unless prevented by some unexpected event —
>
> 2. That one of the Trustees in rotation visit the Academy, one at least each month, to enquire into the conduct of the scholars, the accommodations they have and the government they are subjected to, both in the school and in the families, where they reside. —

Despite the Board's respect and obvious liking for Reverend Smith, matters at the school did not improve. Less than two years later the Trustees received a letter of resignation, a mild and honest document in which the Preceptor gracefully acknowledged failure to come up to the Board's expectations in certain respects, but urging his conscientious concern for the welfare of the school at all times. A brief extract will serve to exemplify the nature of this good old man:

> For want of proper qualifications on my part, or from any other causes, your expectations have not been fulfilled, or the Academy of late years flourished to the degree you could have wished — I can only express my regret. — To perform the duty required of me, so far as I was capable of doing so, inclination has never been wanting, and I cannot persuade myself that during my continuance in this situation, I have at any time been wholly useless . . .

> . . . I would add my earnest wishes, that in the choice of a successor, you may meet with one, whose solicitude to promote the ends, for which this seminary was founded, may be equally sincere and whose endeavors will be more successful.

Reluctantly the Trustees accepted his resignation, requesting that Mr. Smith remain at the school until a successor be found. Evidence of the members' affection for the man who had guided the destinies of the school for eighteen years is spread on the record of their proceedings, expressing in part their appreciation of ". . . those literary qualifications, that amiable temper and that unaffected piety, which, in you, have commanded their love and respect." Their letter to the retiring Preceptor closed with most sincere best wishes for his future welfare. A few months after his departure from the Academy in December of 1809, he assumed the duties of Chaplain to the Poor House in Boston, in which position he lived out his life, his Christian temper earning him once more the deep respect and affection of all those with whom his work brought him in contact.

By the time of the departure of Isaac Smith from the Academy, the appearance of the grounds had undergone several changes. As in Master Moody's day the Mansion House stood sedately some fifty yards to the east of the Bay Road, also called the Old Post Road, the main thoroughfare from Boston north. In all probability the Little Red Schoolhouse had stood closer to the road and somewhat to the right, not far from the now famous Milestone. Whether there was a farmhouse and whether it, too, stood in the vicinity is not clear. A 1786 survey map of the property, now hanging in the Mansion House, shows two buildings

Moody House

(built upon the foundations of Isaac Smith's old home and resembling it closely)

standing north of the Mansion and the schoolhouse, in the general area where the Newbury Memorial stone is now placed. It is likely that these were both barns, as "barns" are referred to several times in the Trustees' records for the period.

An entry in William Bentley's diary, dated March 21, 1793, reads in part:

> . . . rode to the Academy and dined with the Preceptor. The road was very bad . . . & a violent snow storm came on, which lasted all day. The Academy is much repaired, a new white balustrade fence is before the Mansion House. The Old School built for Master Moody, & since a writing school, is neglected . . . [the main classroom] is now cleared for exhibitions. . .

By this time, then, the original schoolhouse was no longer being used as the classroom building. (Indeed, it must have been very small for the large numbers of boys crowded into it under Master Moody.) The second schoolhouse has long since been sold and moved off the Academy property, but still stands nearby, the first building on the right, north of Middle Road on Elm. Just where it stood in the time of Isaac Smith has never been ascertained; it is possible that it may have been on the Mansion House lawn where the third schoolhouse, now Parsons, stood before it was moved to its present location. Record is to be found of repairs made to the Little Red Schoolhouse and to the farm barns in 1795; it may be that the former first came into use as a carriage house at that time. In 1802 the Trustees voted to sell this little building, but fortunately for us who today enjoy it in its beautifully restored state, no buyer was ever found to take it away.

In 1800 Isaac Smith purchased and moved onto the farm, to the spot where Moody House now stands, a house for use as his own residence. Tradition has it that it was this same building which burned in December, 1914, and which was replaced by Moody House; indeed, the present dormitory is said to resemble its predecessor very closely in outside appearance.

In 1806 the Trustees authorized the erection of a big new barn to replace the two outworn structures. In all likelihood, it was built in the same location, "contiguous with the road," where the others had stood before being torn down to make room for it. Thus, by the time of Mr. Smith's resignation the estate boasted — in addition to the old schoolhouse, the Mansion House, and some scattered outbuildings — a second and larger schoolhouse, a very large new barn (which according to school accounts cost a total of $1,394.14 — a highly respectable sum in that day!), and a house belonging to the retiring Preceptor.

One other change in the physical aspect of the property reached completion sometime in the year 1805. The new Turnpike from Newburyport to Boston was extended across the eastern sector of the farm, near the edge of the marshes. Several members of the Board were among the promoters of this highway, authorized in 1803, which reduced the distance from Newburyport to Boston from 43 miles by the winding Old Post Road to 32 miles almost in a straight line. The Trustees received from the Turnpike Corporation payment in consequence of damages sustained to Academy property due to construction of the road. In 1805 the Trustees also entered upon negotiations which resulted in Elm Street's being extended from the point where it met the Old Post Road in front of the Mansion House, eastward through the farm to where it presently reaches the Turnpike.

As for the farm itself, for three or four years after the departure of Joseph Moody, Richard Dummer, a charter member of the Board of Trustees, held the lease, paying the Trust in the neighborhood of ninety-three pounds annually (the actual sum agreed upon for the year 1793). From 1794 through 1798 the lease was held by a tenant who turned out to be unsatisfactory, especially since apparently he did not pay his rent promptly, if at all at the end. From 1798 the farm was occupied and run by Samuel Northend, who remained on excellent terms with the Trust until succeeded by his son John in 1809.

As soon as the Moodys had departed, the Board assumed close supervision over the management of the Academy business, including the farm. (They had, indeed, carefully checked upon Joseph Moody's management from the time of the Act of Incorporation.) Most of the time, responsibility was delegated to a Farm Committee composed of three of the Trustees. Their particular concern, besides overseeing normal upkeep and repair, seems to have been in connection with proper rotation of fields and the judicious cutting of timber and setting out of new trees.

In the last years of the century a long controversy began between the Trustees and one Lemuel Noyes, a near neighbor on the west and south, who occupied a farm on the property where Ambrose House now stands. This stubborn individual persisted in running his cattle across a portion of the Academy land and at one time actually ". . . dug a ditch and erected a stone wall & rail fence across a point of upland and marsh part of the farm belonging to the Trustees . . . & thereby enclosed some land & Marsh belonging to the Trustees with his own land . . ." The disagreement lasted for more than twenty years before being finally settled.

The relationship with other neighbors was apparently amicable. Some, indeed, were members of the Board. As for others, while the new barn was being built, the school paid to board "joiners" at the home of Enoch Boynton, on the Turnpike, a few hundred yards away.

In the latter part of the eighteenth century many private academies of New England turned to their state governments for financial grants. Such grants were not made in cash, but in public lands. Subsidy of this kind had been common from the time of the Revolutionary War, when many soldiers were paid off in this way. In 1793 the Trustees of Dummer Academy applied to the Commonwealth of Massachusetts for such a grant. Following passage by the legislature of an enabling act in 1797, the school received (at the same time as several other academies, including Phillips Academy in Andover) the award of one-half a township in Maine. According to the terms of the grant, it was the responsibility of the grantee to locate and improve the land thus received. This was in itself an expensive process. In addition, there were requirements concerning the number of families to be settled thereon in a given period of time, together with the specification of lots to be set aside for religious and educational purposes.

In 1800 the Trustees succeeded in selling their grant (today part of the town of Woodstock, Maine) in one piece, at the rate of three shillings and threepence per acre, amounting, no doubt, to a healthy sum, though total payment actually spread over a long period of years. The purchaser was one Michael Little of Poland, Maine, who took over the property under the same terms as had been accepted with the grant by the Academy. Unquestionably this was at the time a fortunate stroke of business for the school, for it profited from the grant without having to invest in survey or improvement of the land. Following this successful negotiation, tuition was for a while remitted at the school, and provision was made for the support of a regular Assistant Preceptor at the established salary of $300.00 annually. In the audit of 1806 the holdings of the Academy, exclusive of lands and buildings, were valued at $13,871.33.

It is a bit difficult to estimate the actual salary of the Preceptor during these years. He was entitled to rents, issues and profits of the estate — after the money required to cover "necessary reparation of the estate" had been deducted. In addition, he at various times was granted tuition money, or cash in lieu of tuition. The former ranged from twenty-eight shillings a year per student (for a short time) to twenty-five cents a week from those boys who came from outside of New England (which could scarcely have amounted to a princely sum); the latter was set at $33.33 a quarter, or $133.33 a year.

The dates of vacation separating each of the four quarters varied, dependent upon the date of the Harvard College Commencement. During the latter part of Mr. Smith's tenure, winter vacation was discontinued, and there were three terms instead of four. The vacations came at Thanksgiving time, for two weeks; for two weeks in the spring; and for two weeks in the summer, starting on the Monday prior to the Harvard Commencement — making for a long school year! On the Friday preceding the beginning of summer vacation, an "exhibition" of the students was customarily held at the Academy, at which time those Trustees who wished to might take it upon themselves to question the students in order to ascertain their progress. These dignitaries would meet in the morning for the annual election of officers, lunch at the Mansion House, and then adjourn to the "exhibition," where the pupils would be awaiting them in some trepidation.

By the time of Isaac Smith's withdrawal in 1809, the enrollment at the school had sadly diminished; and the Trustees, while retaining at its height their respect for their old friend, looked anxiously forward to an improvement in conditions at the school under the direction of his successor.

As for the venerable retiring Preceptor, perhaps no more fitting words can be spoken of him than these few quoted from the sermon delivered at his funeral:

"He lived without reproach, honoured and beloved."

CHAPTER IV

Allen, Abbot, and Adams

In the twelve years following the withdrawal of Isaac Smith, the fortunes of Dummer Academy fell victim to so eccentric a sequence of good, and then bad luck as to engender in the minds of her Trustees and her friends high hopes and, ultimately, understandable disappointment. In the first place, Dr. Benjamin Allen, the man whom the Board secured as Preceptor, was a happy choice — though not, indeed, their initial selection. (Offer of the post had been first accepted, and then rejected by the Reverend Jacob Abbot, minister in Hampton Falls, who changed his mind when the members of his parish, seeing that they were in grave danger of losing him, found a solution to the disagreements which had caused his determination to resign.)

Dr. Allen had been a highly respected Professor at Union College in Schenectady, New York. Upon leaving Union, he had originally planned to start a school of his own ". . . in order to lay out his talents to more advantage, that is profit, as well as usefulness to the public than his present situation admits," to quote one of the references submitted in his behalf. His friends thought the position at Dummer ready-made for him and supplied the Trustees with the highest of recommendations. Such men as President Nott of Union College and Chief Justice Kent of New York wrote concerning him; John Thornton Kirkland and J. S. Buckminster, President and Lecturer respectively at Harvard College, added their praise. Dr. Allen was present at the Academy on October 22, 1809, the day of his election, to accept his appointment in person.

The Preceptor's salary was set at $800 per annum, together with the use of the Mansion House for his rather considerable family and some boarders, and including, of course, provision of garden space and some of the outbuildings. (Dr. Allen did not accept an alternative offer of $400 anually together with the lease of the Academy farm; Mr. John Northend, the current tenant, remained, and the former home of Preceptor Smith, which had been purchased by the Academy, came into use as the farmhouse.) Once again, so far had the school's fortunes declined in the last years under Mr. Smith, that decision was reached to charge tuition, except to those pupils whose homes were in the Parish of Byfield.

It is not at any point clear when or how Byfield residents were first exempted from paying to attend Dummer School. There is nothing to such effect in the Act of Incorporation. Presumably the custom took root in the widely known generosity of Master Moody and took root so stubbornly as never to be successfully altered, though efforts to eliminate it were made several times during the nineteenth century. The school under Dr. Allen opened on December 26, 1809.

Nehemiah Cleaveland's friendship with Benjamin Apthorp Gould, who was a student at Dummer during Dr. Allen's short tenure, has resulted in first-hand testimony to the new Master's vigorous and thorough management, which immediately began to restore the fortunes of the school. (Mr. Gould, as Principal of Boston Latin School, was to become one of the most distinguished leaders of his day in secondary education. He later served for many years as a Trustee of the Academy.) Enrollment quickly increased from the bare handful of youths under Mr. Smith to twenty-five or more, necessitating the procuring of an assistant to instruct in writing and arithmetic. Mr. Cleaveland quotes one of Dr. Allen's students (probably Mr. Gould):

> I began to translate Greek with Dr. Allen, and from the first lesson to the last, was obliged to learn every thing about every word of every lesson. The effect of his thoroughness was what every good scholar would expect. From thus getting a perfectly exact knowledge as far as I went, I learned to love Greek better than any other study, and have retained the affection to this day. The sufficient reason was, I made a better beginning in it, than in anything else, and *what* I learned I learned better than I ever learned anything before.

There may well be some question as to whether such exactness will inevitably engender in all pupils a lasting attachment to their subject, but such, at least in this case, was Benjamin Allen's successful formula.

The Trustees were justifiably pleased, not only by the record of the school under the new Preceptor, but also because his enthusiasm for and love of teaching (which had, indeed, been alluded to in his recommendations) gave promise of even better days to come. The Board in due time not only voted to authorize the providing of an assistant, but also made plans to put an addition on the Mansion House for the convenience of Dr. Allen's family. But their hopes were dashed. After just a year and nine months of success at the Academy, Benjamin Allen apparently saw an opening elsewhere which might better afford him an opportunity "to lay out his talents to more advantage," for he submitted a letter of resignation on September 21, 1811, "in consequence of a recent appointment." The Trustees reluctantly accepted the resignation, at the same time expressing ". . . their grateful sense of the benefit the Academy has received from his exertions and their best wishes for his future success and prosperity."

The vacancy created by the sudden departure of Dr. Allen was surprisingly short-lived. The Trustees had obviously been somewhat forewarned, for on the same day that they accepted the resignation, they voted to appoint to the Preceptorship the Reverend Abiel Abbot, recently of Connecticut, under the same terms as those enjoyed by his predecessor. Two weeks later Mr. Abbot was officially inducted into office.

At first flush the new appointment looked as promising as had the last. Mr. Abbot was an alumnus of Andover, where his Principal had been the formidable Eliphalet Pearson. After graduating from Harvard in 1787, he had taught at both Harvard and at Andover. In 1795 he was ordained a minister in the church of Coventry, Connecticut, and there he remained until just before coming to Byfield.

The severance of his long connection with the parish in Coventry had resulted from a disagreement stemming from the Reverend Abbot's "heretical opinions," as Nehemiah Cleaveland termed them. His cause aroused some sympathy in his native state of Massachusetts and brought him to the attention of the Trustees. These worthy gentlemen must have felt some considerable satisfaction at procuring the services of so well qualified a man, and one who had stood steadfastly by his convictions, for they had but too recently been witness to what could happen to a school when the hand at the helm lacked firmness. Alas, however, Preceptor Abbot shared the same gentle and amiable nature as Isaac Smith; indeed, it may have been this quality, as much as his theological tenets, which had prompted his departure from his living in Connecticut: his "heretical opinions" appear, in fact, to have been an unwillingness to accept the harsh doctrine of infant damnation.

Once again, this time for eight years, the Preceptor of Dummer Academy was a kindly, scholarly gentleman who could accomplish much with those boys who were gifted and ambitious (Chief Justice

John Searle Tenney of the Supreme Court of Maine got his early training under him). His weakness in discipline, nevertheless, was reflected in a decline once more in enrollment. Never large during his tenure, it grew steadily smaller.

During these years the responsibilities of the Trustees were often heavy. The school was not prospering. Legal steps had to be taken to conclude arrangements made years before when the half township awarded them by the Commonwealth had been disposed of. The purchaser had apparently failed to keep up his payments. Again there was trouble with neighbor Lemuel Noyes, with whom the boundary disagreement had begun way back in the 'nineties. (The Trustees themselves were not proof to error, however, for according to the records they intended in 1812 to reimburse a Mrs. Broomfield for her "Iron Stove," which they were using in the schoolhouse; and in 1817 they were still in possession of this valuable article — and still expressing good intentions of paying poor Mrs. Broomfield for it.) Their pleasant relationships with the Northend family were temporarily broken in 1814 when John, the tenant, was attracted to a new farming venture elsewhere; and the new tenants had not worked out. Such were the problems facing the Board in the summers of 1817 and 1818.

The most immediate problem, however, was the need for replacing Abiel Abbot. This pleasant, friendly man and able scholar submitted his resignation in August, 1817, to become effective the following April. A large number of applications were received in response to the Board's advertisement for a successor, one of them from the recent alumnus John Searle Tenney. Many of the aspirants came highly recommended, and it is a credit both to the qualities of the successful candidate, Samuel Adams, and the perspicacity of the Board that the choice fell upon whom it did. On April 6, 1819, Samuel Adams was elected Preceptor for one year, at a salary of $600 in addition to whatever tuition he might take in (thus tying the salary to the enrollment).

On April 12, six days later, Mr. Adams submitted the following communication to the Trustees:

> To the Standing Committee of the Trustees of Dummer Academy.
>
> Gentlemen,
>
> In reply to the propositions, you were pleased to make to me of this date, relative to my recent appointment

as Preceptor of said institution, I beg leave to state, that I cannot consistently with my present views & feelings acceed to them. I would further observe that I shall be willing to accept of the appointment for one year at least on condition, of the buildings being put in suitable repair, during the ensuing summer;—that the school should be recommenced on the first of Oct. next or near that time, and that I receive substantially, as an annual compensation, the same amount, that the last Preceptor in said Academy has received, viz; the rent of the mansion house together with the garden and outbuildings, that are usually considered as belonging to the same; — a right in the barn for the accommodation of a horse and cow; — and eight hundred dollars, payable quarterly . . .

The letter concludes by indicating that if at the end of a year the Trustees and the Preceptor were mutually satisfied, he would undoubtedly be willing to continue longer in the position.

To these wise conditions the gentlemen of the Board agreed, and in the ensuing months repairs and improvements were made to the Academy property. Chief among these improvements was the substitution for the second schoolhouse, which had been the chief classroom building since the early 1790's, of a new schoolbuilding, one which even today, though moved from its original position and much remodeled, stands as Parsons Schoolhouse. When first built the new structure occupied a prominent place in the center of the Mansion House lawn, somewhat south and west, about two-thirds of the way towards where the Old Bay Road had passed. The front of the building and the bell tower faced on the road.

Before the school was ready for another opening day under a new Preceptor, the Trustees took one more significant step: they adopted and spread upon the record an imposing set of "Bye Laws & Regulations" for the Academy, thirty of them in all. In these were set down guiding principles for both Preceptor and pupils. In general, the Preceptor was made responsible for the guidance of his charges, most especially with respect to their religious and moral training, and he was empowered to devise further regulations towards the accomplishing of these ends, subject to the approval of the Trustees.

With respect to the students, rules were set down pertinent to their qualifying for entrance, as well as to the conduct required of the young gentlemen — and that which might well lead toward expulsion. The curriculum was outlined as follows:

8th   In the Academy shall be taught the proper and grace-ful reading of English . . . English grammar, the Latin and Greek languages, writing and arithmetic, composi-tion, the art of speaking, practical geometry, geography, logic, ethics, the evidences of Christianity, with such other branches of useful and polite education as the Trustees may direct.

Two other "Bye Laws" deserve specific notice at this point, as well for the fact that they reflect the general tone of the whole list, as for the quaintness of their phrasing:

9th   On monday mornings the scholars shall give some account of the sermon they have heard the preceding day, or recite from the bible, or some other religious books, such lessons as may have been previously assign-ed.

11th   Walking for amusement in the streets or fields on the sabbath, with everything else in conversation or con-duct inconsistent with the solemnity of the day, is strictly forbidden.

"No ball, stick or stone" was to be thrown by any scholar so as to endanger any of the Academy property, and damage thus created was to be paid for by the culprits, a familiar precept to students of our own day. Nor were the boys to walk on the property of any of the neighbors or pick "fruit" from the gardens or orchards without permission. Class hours from the first of April until the first of October were set at from 8:00 A.M. until noon, and from 2:00 until 6:00 P.M. The rest of the year, during the period of cold weather and early darkness, the hours were shortened by one hour at either end of the day. On Wednesday and Saturday afternoons school was recessed. There were four vacations during the year, in February, May, August and November, each for two weeks. It was stipulated that the entire list of regulations was to be read to the students "as often as once every term."

Once again matters looked hopeful. The school was to reopen under the most favorable circumstances. Mr. Adams, the new Pre-ceptor, a graduate of Harvard College in 1806, had taught for a number of years in nearby Salem, before becoming a successful businessman. He was highly respected in the area, and at the time of his acceptance of the post at the Academy he was a senator-elect to the Massachusetts legislature. In addition, the physical plant at the school was newly refurbished and enlarged. These circumstances became widely known and contributed to the fact that twenty-eight boys, the same number which had greeted Master Moody in his first year, stood ready to enter upon the reopening of the institution. The outlook was auspicious.

Less favorable omen could be drawn from the fact that the start of the new term, already postponed so that the new building might be completed, was further delayed by the ill health of Mr. Adams. Nevertheless, classes commenced under favorable circumstances on the eleventh of April, 1820. In the following year the enrollment climbed rapidly until at one time it totaled almost fifty. (In 1820 and 1821 sixty-six boys came to Dummer to study under Samuel Adams and his assistant, more than half the number that had studied under the two preceding preceptors over a period of ten years.)

Of the Exhibition in August 1821, the Reverend John Andrews, Secretary to the Board, reported:

> The Trustees were engaged in the morning by attending an examination of the Students and also an exhibition of their speaking, in both of which exercises they appeared to very great advantage and much to the honor of their Instructors. —

At the same meeting the Trustees were obliged to consider what to do concerning a letter of resignation submitted with regret by Mr. Adams. It reads in part:

> It is with painful emotions that I feel myself reduced to the necessity of communicating to you . . . my wish to resign the office I now hold in this institution. If this measure should occasion disappointment to any, I believe none will feel it to be such more sensibly than myself . . .

The rigors of managing a school growing so quickly in popularity had been too much for the Preceptor's delicate health. Although in order to allow the Trustees time to seek a successor, he had acceded to their request that he remain for another few weeks after the vacation, he was never able to carry out his intention. Hardly more than two weeks after his wife had written from Dorchester, in October, 1821, expressing in part her husband's regret over his enforced absence from the school, word was received of Mr. Adams's death. He was but thirty-seven years old.

Thus, within only twelve years the fortunes of the Academy had blossomed with promise three separate times, and each time they had suffered blight. During this same period Phillips Academy at Andover was growing steadily in strength under the firm hand of John Adams, while at Exeter the long and productive tenure of Benjamin Abbot was advancing strongly at midcareer. Dummer Academy, the oldest of the three venerable schools, had fallen sadly behind, and though there were better days ahead, it was to be many long years before she could recover her full momentum.

CHAPTER V

Nehemiah Cleaveland

Samuel Adams, to oblige the Trustees, had originally agreed to extend his stay at the Academy from the date of his resignation in August, 1821, until October 11. When it became clear that he was unable to carry on, the school reconvened under the supervision of his assistant, Mr. Taylor G. Worcester. The Trustees in general were apparently in accord with one of their number, the Reverend Elijah Parish, who wrote that it was ". . . important that a Preceptor should immediately occupy the premises . . ." Promptly on the eleventh of October, therefore, Nehemiah Cleaveland was inducted into office. Once again the Board was fortunate in its selection; for nineteen years Mr. Cleaveland was to provide firm, vigorous, and intelligent leadership. Yet a perverse fortune must have ordained that his very success should lay the foundation of ultimate disappointment. The Academy, like the son of Daedalus, exulted too much in its progress and in attempting to soar too high contributed to its own downfall. Nevertheless, credit for the progress, not blame for the downfall, belongs to Nehemiah.

Twenty-five boys made up the population of the school upon Mr. Cleaveland's arrival. Though the Trustees had voted to provide an assistant when the number topped thirty, the Preceptor, in spite of rapid increase beyond this figure, did not for some years see fit to take advantage of the authorization. Instead he made use of the more talented older boys to help with the tutelage of the younger, arranging that the tuition charge for his student-assistants be remitted in return for their efforts.

In the next nineteen years, of the more than 400 boys who came there to study, a total of 360 graduated from Dummer Academy. Such success prompted the Trustees to investigate extensively a number of plans "for increasing the usefulness of the school." The first called for the creation of an agricultural department which was to be endowed jointly by the Academy and the Commonwealth of Massachusetts. The Dummer Farm did, indeed, offer a promising site for such an experiment. For a time prospects for the addition appeared good, but in the end they failed. Hope was revived a few years later (in 1834) and once more faltered.

47

For some reason unknown to Mr. Cleaveland the agricultural project had met with disfavor among the inhabitants of Byfield, and for a brief while his relations with the parish were strained (though the suggested change was neither his, nor particularly popular with him).

In later years there developed an ill-fated move to divide the Academy into two departments: Classical, as it had always been, and English — each under its own Master, each Master with equal authority. (It was this move which was ultimately responsible for the Preceptor's resignation.) There was, finally, the effort to interest the Legislature and others in attaching to the Academy a teacher-training school. Each of the plans for expansion found its source in the sound progress of the school under the leadership of Nehemiah Cleaveland. The Preceptor himself did not favor attempts to change the status quo; particularly did he disapprove the plan which was actually adopted. He felt that he understood the natural limitations of the institution, and he was loath to see them exceeded. The seat of the school was relatively remote. He did not share the confidence evinced by a committee of the Trust, which submitted in 1838 an opinion that about one hundred students could be suitably accommodated within one-half mile or less of the Academy. (On campus at this time there was still only the Mansion House for the accommodation of boys, though the Preceptor had moved his family into the house newly constructed for his use — now the "Commons" dormitory.)

For one who reads between the lines in Mr. Cleaveland's *Centennial Discourse,* in his letters to his friend Professor Alpheus Packard at Bowdoin, and in all references to him elsewhere, it becomes evident that the new head of Dummer Academy was a gifted and dedicated teacher, a man of determination and strength, of severity when necessary, but withal a man of understanding and warm wit. His portrait reflects dignity, self-possession, and an unflinching gaze — yet with a hint of humor in the eyes and in the lines of the face. Nor does it hide the asperity which could be loosed without stint on those who failed to come up to the mark. Of one ambitious Trustee whose zealous, but misguided efforts in behalf of the school met with his disapproval, Nehemiah wrote tartly :

> . . . To him, as I have always supposed, the Academy and the public are mainly indebted for the experimental project and double-headed arrangement of 1837. If

so, he is justly entitled to a liberal share of whatever praise is due to that unfortunate enterprise.

He was a man to call a spade a spade, but into his punctilious style there constantly crept a human warmth and simplicity. When Professor Packard wrote to congratulate him on his *Centennial Discourse,* he replied:

> Your approbation of my Byfield preachment is truly gratifying . . . For a moment, I was, perhaps, in danger of being puffed up. The peril was momentary only and I am now quite calm.

Nehemiah's wit remained sharp and his handwriting precise until the day of his death in the middle of his eighty-first year.

Mr. Cleaveland, who had been brought up in nearby Topsfield and who had studied briefly under old Isaac Smith at Dummer, was amply qualified to assume leadership of the school. He had entered Bowdoin in 1809, at the age of thirteen, graduating with the Class of 1812. In the years immediately following he studied theology, taught school (for three years he was a tutor at his own college in Brunswick), and began the study of medicine. This last undertaking ended when he accepted his election as Preceptor at Dummer. In Latin and Greek he was an accomplished scholar, and his knowledge of chemistry led him to present a widely attended series of lectures on that subject in Newburyport in 1830. In addition, his letters, frequently interspersed with learned quotations (sometimes in French, as well as Latin and Greek), give evidence of thorough scholarship and wide intellectual curiosity concerning the issues of his day. During and after the Civil War he was an ardent Grant man (but emphatically not an enthusiast for Greeley, Charles Francis Adams, or General Benjamin Butler):

> . . . I have faith in Grant — faith in Meade — faith in the brave men whom they command — above all, faith in a just cause and righteous Providence.
>
> I think as you [Professor Packard] do in regard to the folly of placing Butler in high military command . . .

This sturdy Yankee — august in aspect, yet human; exacting, yet understanding — had a steadying influence which inspired confidence in all who were associated with the Academy. In the words of one commentator ". . . . it was allowed by common consent that the mantle of Master Moody, which had so long been suspended in mid-air, had at last fallen on his shoulders." His own words best describe the school as he knew it:

> I found here a bright, pleasant set of scholars, which soon increased. Severe as the first season was, I still recall with pleasure my first winter here. With five years of experience as an instructor in schools and in College, the cares and duties of teaching were not new to me. But the position brought other cares and unwonted responsibilities. My appointment had been accompanied with a special request of the Trustees that I should have a family, and open the Mansion-House to as many of my pupils as it would accommodate. It was an arrangement, which, in the paucity of boarding houses, seemed almost essential to the prosperity of the school. But with it, of necessity, came also a large additional care. Fortunate the teacher, who can dismiss his solicitudes when he dismisses his school.

Mr. Cleaveland (who was fortunately already provided with a family to comply with the injunctions of the Board!) pays heartfelt tribute to his good wife, who with him had to share the regulating of a houseful of lively boys. And he earnestly commends the conjugal estate to succeeding headmasters:

> In a spot so retired and so exempt from the excitements of life — amid a community uncommonly sparse and not eminently social, — the Principal of Dummer Academy should have a home that will keep him busy and happy, if he would drive away the surly demon of discontent.

Several events during Nehemiah Cleaveland's tenure, some already alluded to briefly, played key parts in the variable fortunes of the school. Practically throughout Mr. Cleaveland's preceptorship, and sporadically thereafter, an alumni body known as the Sons of Dummer made significant contributions to the well-being of the Academy. Established in the summer of 1822 under the joint auspices of the Preceptor and the Honorable Dudley Atkins Tyng (a pupil at the school under Master Moody and a Trustee for thirteen years), it was incorporated in 1833. This society, created in part ". . . to promote and extend the usefulness and reputation of the Academy . . . ," awarded prizes to deserving scholars and from time to time loaned or gave sums of money for needed improvements at the school. Of the nearly one hundred members in its early years, more than one-half had been students under Master Moody.

In addition to Mr. Tyng, the Board at this time included several long-term and loyal members, among them the Reverend John Andrews, who was in his fourth decade of membership, still serving both as Secretary and Treasurer. Judge Samuel S. Wilde was President of the body, and Elijah Parish, Silas Little (a conscientious member of the Farm Committee), Deacon Daniel Hale (about whom more later), and Ebenezer Moseley were in the midst of long tenures. The steadily improving fortunes of the Academy encouraged these gentlemen and their confreres to investigate the prospects of attaching an agricultural school to the Academy, consulting successively the officials of the Massachusetts State Agricultural Society and of the Commonwealth, with the final result already described. For a time the plan looked promising (so much so that the Trust gave the Farm tenant three months' notice), but in the end no action was taken. The Trustees' records reflect for several months thereafter a strained relationship between the school and its neighbors. To ease some of the tension there was a vote in 1826 to keep the boys in school on Wednesday afternoons instead of following the usual recess, though the Preceptor was empowered to grant an afternoon off "on special occasions . . . as a reward for diligence and good conduct." Apparently the high-spirited scholars did not contribute to harmonious community relations at this unsettled time.

The Academy continued to prosper in a modest way. In the summer of 1830 the holdings of the school (exclusive of buildings and grounds) had a value in excess of $15,000. In 1831 such was the financial situation that the Board voted to reduce tuition charges and empowered the Preceptor to "remit the tuition in behalf of any deserving pupils . . . whose circumstances require it . . ." Meanwhile a committee was studying the possibility of operating entirely as a "free school" and considering the expedience of employing an assistant should the enrollment exceed forty. At the annual Exhibition for that year a highly commendatory entry appears in the minutes:

> The Trustees attended an examination of the students in the Academy and were highly pleased with the evidences which the pupils gave of their improvement; with their correct and respectable appearance in the various studies in which they had been engaged. They reflected honor upon themselves and their Preceptor.

The actions responsible for the sudden reversal of good times are best described in Nehemiah Cleveland's own words:

> In 1836, I suggested to some of the Trustees the idea of erecting another dwelling-house on the Academy grounds; — partly to provide more accommodation for the boarding of pupils — but especially as a means of securing for the school a permanent Assistant. It was my belief — and I have seen no reason to change it — that an expenditure, to this end, of some $2,000 or $3,000 of the fund, which was then in good condition, would be a profitable investment for the Academy. The proposition was well received, but unfortunately it gave rise to visions of improvement and of greatness much too fine to be realized. They would reorganize the school. There would be an English Department and an English teacher independent of and co-equal with the Classical. There would be some outlay at first — but the augmented expense would be more than met by the enlarged attendance which was to result from the new arrangement.
>
> They did me the honor to ask my opinion of the plan. Years of experience and observation on the spot had qualified me to form some estimate of the probable success of the project, and I felt sure that Dummer Academy had in store, no such future as imagination seemed to have spread before the eyes of those gentlemen. My doubts were not concealed. But it was decided that the experiment should go on. Accordingly, a new house was erected — the old mansion was altered and refitted — and a Teacher of good repute was put at the head of the English Department.

Such were the frank views of the Preceptor, who had had more than fifteen years at the Academy in which to form them. The average association of the Trustees with the school, exclusive of Mr. Andrews, was less than eight years. The move to expand the program was spearheaded by the newer members of the Board, whose ambitions for the Academy, if ill-advised, are at least understandable. Judge Wilde had retired as their President, and the Honorable Ebenezer Moseley served in his stead. He and a handful of his more experienced colleagues were swayed by the enthusiasm of their newer associates, who saw the school as

THE COMMONS (LEFT) AND PARSONS SCHOOLHOUSE (1950)

standing somewhat in the shade of her more favored sisters, like Exeter and Andover:

> . . . It is an old Institution, its' [sic] funds are still in being, undiminished by waste or perversion, it has still an able Instructor, a valuable library, a competent number of scholars, convenient buildings and all the facilities for imparting a good education and sound morals, and the Board of Trustees would hope that they can confidently say for themselves that they feel an undiminished desire to raise this Institution to that first rank of usefulness for which its venerable benefactor designed it. . .

Thus wrote the investigating committee to the full Board. They appended a list of seven recommendations intended to implement their plans for two departments in the school. Then they went on to add:

> Before closing, the Committee must be allowed to say they cannot but indulge a strong hope and belief that the ancient renown of this venerable Academy, its beautiful situation, its large endowments, the design of its benevolent founder, the eminent men which it has sent forth into the world, and the healthful powers which it still retains justify us in incurring some hazards and expenses to make it more extensively useful . . .

The plan was put into motion. A new dwelling was erected south of the Mansion House; the latter was once more made over to accommodate boarders. Nehemiah moved his family into the the new building, which, much enlarged, stands today as Commons dormitory. Supervision of the Mansion was assumed by the leader, "a Teacher of good repute," of the new English Department, Mr. Phineas Nichols of Portsmouth, New Hampshire. The new order was established — and confirmed in August, 1837, when the Reverends Leonard Withington and Thomas Fox, among the newest Trustees in point of service, were elected President and Vice-President, respectively, of the Board. Within three years the three Trustees of longest standing had retired: Deacon Daniel Hale (1815-1837); John Andrews (1789-1838), just one year short of fifty years a Trustee; and the resigned President, Ebenezer Moseley (1815-1839).

As Preceptor Cleaveland had anticipated, under the new arrangement the "enlarged attendance" fell far short of the expectations of the Board. The fund of the Academy, already depleted by the repairs and additions to the Academy plant, melted away quickly under the necessity of supporting two Teachers, with little increase in income. The situation was greatly aggravated by the reaction of Byfield Parish to a decision of the Board at the time of the change-over. This decision was to institute a charge to students attending the Academy from Byfield, one-half the regular tuition rate. The folk of Byfield were incensed. From the very first their children had attended Dummer free of any charge. In vain did the Trustees point out that nowhere in the Governor's Will was there any evidence of intent to provide free education. Children of Byfield residents were withdrawn from their classes, increasing the enrollment problem. Once more, relations in the community were tense. The Board unsuccessfully attempted compromise, offering to permit to Byfielders free education in the Classical Department, if full tuition were paid in the English Department. Finally, after almost two years of squabbling, tuition to children from the parish was set at one-quarter of the regular rate, and some parents returned their offspring to classes.

Meanwhile a "Prudential Committee" of the Board was established to supervise the internal affairs of the Academy in an attempt to keep the Trustees in closer touch with the management of the school, this committee to report to the full Board at the annual meeting. Mr. Withington, very active in the affairs of the Trust for the past seven years, resigned his Presidency and his membership, the Reverend Mr. Fox, a member of five years' standing, being elected to replace him in office. The records for this time clearly reflect the beginning of financial difficulties. Close inquiries were instituted into the possibility of attaching to the Academy a normal school, authorized and partially subsidized by the Board of Education of the Commonwealth. The Sons of Dummer offered substantial monetary support for the project, and the Board went so far as to authorize its President to consult with Horace Mann concerning the undertaking. The plan for such a school was never activated.

By 1840 it was clear that matters had reached a serious pass. A committee was assigned to investigate the financial situation and consult with Mr. Cleaveland and Mr. Nichols. Invited to confer with the Trustees, Nehemiah Cleaveland did not wait:

> As the shortest method of solving the problem I sent in my resignation. The step was one which I could then take without reluctance and without great regret. Byfield

had been a pleasant home, but I had lived there long enough. The ill-judged alteration in the constitution of the Academy had spoiled it for me, and I was rather thankful than otherwise for a decent pretext to retire.

This resignation, obviously, was greeted with dismay by the Trustees, but the Preceptor's mind, "after much and calm reflection on the subject," was made up. There was nothing for the Board to do but to accept. On the motion of the Reverend Henry Durant, Byfield Parish minister and thereby (in accordance with the tradition which began with Moses Parsons) a member of the Trust, there was conveyed to Mr. Cleaveland "the high sense entertained by the Board of his talents & requirements as a scholar, his character as a gentleman, & of the value of his services as a teacher for so many years in the Academy under their care, & also . . . the best wishes of the Board for his success & happiness in whatever sphere of labor he may be called to Enter."

Before following, from this point, the fortunes of an Academy once again — and suddenly — become insecure, it would be well to speak briefly of a few of the men who during his nineteen years at Dummer were closely associated with Nehemiah Cleaveland. Tenant of the farm during the whole of Mr. Cleaveland's preceptorship, and for eleven years thereafter, was the same John Northend (returned from five years of farming elsewhere) who had succeeded his father in that capacity in 1809. Mr. Northend managed the Farm and occupied the farmhouse for a total of thirty-seven years, providing in that time good board for many Academy students. Of his ten children, several graduated from the Academy. One son, Charles, was for a time a regular assistant to Mr. Cleaveland, before moving on to a valuable and active career in public education. Another, William Dummer Northend, was a lawyer, a state senator, and for twenty-six years a member of the Board of Trustees of the Academy.

No history of Dummer would be complete without some account of Deacon Daniel Hale. His entire life was lived in close conjunction with the Academy. For thirty-one years, from 1786 until 1817, his father, Joseph, had served as a Trustee, taking much of the responsibility for supervision of the Farm, and receiving into his home (now the property of the Academy, located across Middle Road from the Alumni Gymnasium) many of the boys at the school. In all, the Hales, father and son, served one-half a century on the Board, for Daniel was elected to membership two years before his father's retirement and remained until 1837. He, too, was an important member of the Farm Committee, and his home remained, next to the Mansion House, the chief resort of boarding students. "For some thirty years," reports Nehemiah, "Mr. Hale took boys to board and many and sore were the trials which they brought him. I hope they long since repented of the pranks which tried the good man's temper, as he, I am sure, soon forgave and quite forgot them." Many are the anecdotes told of the long-suffering Squire. Dr. Ewell, in his *The Story of Byfield*, points out that the Academy lacked a gymnasium in those days, ". . . and the scholars seem to have vented their youthful exuberance of physical spirit on the good Deacon's windows and furniture." In Mr. Hale's account book appears, among others similar, the following entry:

Glass   March 1836
. . . G. Choate one pane Mch 31
Robert Codman 3 at one time on purpose
Arthur Gilman one 6¼ cts
    "   "   and W. Codman one between them
Charles Wood 3 panes
Arthur Gilman to breaking one chair

At a reunion in 1847 ex-culprit Arthur Gilman, by that time a distinguished scholar, proposed the following toast: "The memory of Daniel Hale, Esq., who, although bored by boys for forty-five years [sic], still for forty-five years unflinchingly took boys to board."

Finally, a word should be said of Mr. Phineas Nichols, who unwittingly became a part of the disaster which followed in the wake of the division of the school in 1837. The first and only head of the English Department, he was apparently a friendly, able, and conscientious man. Nehemiah Cleaveland clearly liked him and characterized him as "assiduous and faithful" in discharge of his duty, and credited him as well with making the Mansion House a good home for the boys. Certainly the ill fortune of the Academy during his tenure could in no way be accounted to him.

Though following his resignation in 1840, Mr. Cleaveland departed to teach elsewhere (at Phillips Exeter Academy; in Lowell, Massachusetts; and for five years at his own "very pleasant school for young ladies in Brooklyn, New York"), Dummer Academy had not yet received the last of his good offices. This vigorous and able man was to become for the eleven years prior to his death in 1877 an active and valuable member of the Board of Trustees. In her letter to his friend Professor Packard, following her father's death, Nehemiah's daughter described the old teacher as "humble, trusting, and resigned at the end," his mind absolutely clear to the last.

CHAPTER VI

F. A. Adams, Durant, and Chute

The actions of the Trustees during 1836 and 1837 clearly laid too heavy a burden upon the economic structure of the school. The cost of building the "new dwelling" for the Preceptor and his family was slightly more than $3,000. Extensive repairs to the Mansion House and schoolhouse, and the enclosing of the campus by a fence amounted to almost $1,000 more. New books were purchased to augment the library of the Academy, which according to the Trustees' records already "spread a literary feast before the tasteful student" (though it still contained little more than the books originally contributed from Governor Dummer's library almost 100 years previous). The addition of a Teacher for the English Department almost doubled the cost of instruction.

The Board had extended its lines too far: the anticipated increase in enrollment, with a concomitant addition to the receipts from tuition, failed to materialize. In fact, with Byfield youngsters withdrawn by parents resisting a tuition charge to local residents, enrollment temporarily dropped, and following Mr. Cleaveland's resignation in 1840 it dropped again.

In August, 1838, the Prudential Committee in its report included the following optimistic note:

> . . . notwithstanding the state of the times and the great expense to which the Trustees have been subjected, they see much to encourage them in the new regulations — The Teachers are able faithful men; they have devoted themselves to their work; the progress of the pupils has been good . . . and the Academy seems to be rising gradually into notice and gaining upon the public confidence and patronage. It only wants the fostering care of some diligent men who can afford to give it a large place in their time and attention; to watch over it with paternal care; to visit often; to recommend it by precept and example; and bear it in their affections and prayers to his blessing and protection from whom comes each sacred endeavor and all final success.

At this very meeting, apparently finding himself unable to give to the Academy "large place" in his time and attention, President of the Board Leonard Withington resigned his membership. Reverend Withington, a relatively new member (and Chairman of the Prudential Committee which wrote the report from which the excerpt just quoted was taken) had been a leader in the recent revisions. Elected to succeed him as President of the Trust was the Reverend Thomas Fox, another of the ambitious younger members.

For fifteen years, with scarcely more than its regular annual meetings for the purposes of attending an examination of the students and to deal with necessary business arrangements, the Board had left the running of the Academy in the hands of Nehemiah Cleaveland. Under his guidance the school had achieved and maintained a modest prosperity, but one, in the view of the Preceptor, suiting well with its character and its circumstances. It may well be that what the institution needed was not to be watched over with "paternal care" by a solicitous committee of the Trust, but rather to be allowed, without interference, the continued wise ministrations of Nehemiah.

Be that how it may, by 1840 the school was in trouble financially. Mr. Cleaveland departed with mixed feelings of regret and relief. The new "two-headed" arrangement tottered. With the whole country still suffering the effects of the economic panic which followed Andrew Jackson's second term as President, times did not favor a rapid recovery by the school. There followed twelve years of rocky going as the Trustees tried to retrench. It is likely, therefore, that the school's plight during this period was more the consequence of economic insecurity than of any fault in the men called upon to fill the gap left by Nehemiah Cleaveland.

The division of the Academy into Classical and English Departments under separate leadership ended in the fall of 1840. The Trustees passed a motion to have only one Teacher again, and an Assistant. The experiment was over. Although it was still possible to register either for Classical or English studies (or, now, a combination of the two), the administration of the school rested in the hands of a single head. Mr. Phineas Nichols remained for a short time as Assistant, in charge of the English curriculum. Mr. Frederic A. Adams had been retained to take charge of the Academy.

Mr. Cleaveland could at least take pleasure in the new appointment, for Frederic Adams had been one of his finest student-assistants at Dummer. When Adams arrived, as Nehemiah explained in the *Centennial Discourse,* the Academy ". . . was still laboring under its self-imposed burden, and although that soon dropped off from general weakness, the weakness itself remained." He continued:

> Notwithstanding the untoward circumstances I have mentioned, The Academy, during the greater part of Mr. Adams' continuance, was well attended; its instruction in every branch was comprehensive and thorough; and its discipline, though mild, was efficient. That his services as a teacher here were exceedingly valuable, and generally acceptable not only to the Trustees, but to his pupils and their parents, I have every reason to believe.

Despite the hopes of the Trustees and the presence of competent and conscientious teachers, the school found itself for an extended period becalmed in efforts to make ends meet and still keep the Academy afloat. Enrollment suffered until in February of 1845 a committee was appointed to confer with Mr. Adams ". . . as to what measures may be adopted for the increase of the number of pupils and the diminution of the expenses of the Board." In August, 1846, only twenty-five scholars presented themselves for the annual examination by the Trustees, who, nevertheless, adjudged the young men's performances "highly gratifying."

Meanwhile the Board was plagued with other problems. A farmer neighbor, Paul Pillsbury, persisted in trespassing on property which the Trustees considered theirs. Not until 1849 was agreement finally reached, by means of a survey, concerning ownership of pastureland and responsibility for fences. In addition, a series of skirmishes were taking place between the Prudential Committee and various lessees of Academy property. Even John Northend, long the valued tenant of the Farm, had differences with the Board. The times were not auspicious.

For those boys in the school, however, the pursuit of an education continued unabated — and not entirely without excitement. An entertaining reminiscence by Nathan N. Withington, who attended the Academy from 1845 to 1847, appears in the February, 1903, issue of the *Dummer News.* Mr. Withington, somewhat older than his classmates at the Academy, had an interest in a young lady, the daughter of a farmer who lived some three

DUMMER ACADEMY (CIRCA 1844)

miles from the Academy. He recalls with pleasure the fortunate predilection of the boy who was responsible for ringing the 9:00 P. M. curfew bell to postpone that unpopular duty as long as he conveniently could:

> One evening that winter I left the house of the girl I was courting just as their clock struck nine. The house was near the Oldtown end of the Four Rock bridge road, and I ran the whole length of the road to the Turnpike, when the Newburyport bells, according to the custom of that time, rang for nine o'clock. I continued running along the Turnpike, and passed the Academy just as the nine o'clock bell began to ring, and got inside Capt. Noyes's door before it ceased.
>
> Now it was clearly impossible . . . to run three miles and a half or more in no time. The family where I had been calling were farmers, and they are apt to keep their clocks considerably fast. The town bells were doubtless pretty nearly on the correct time and of course the Academy boy was reprehensibly slow, if time is money, though he seemed to me a very amicable, accommodating fellow.

Shortly afterward Mr. Withington left the boarding house of Captain Daniel Noyes (so unfortunately gutted by fire in 1958, but since rebuilt) to live at home, walking the four miles to school with two companions, the three of them often conjugating Greek verbs or declining adjectives as they went.

Shortly after the demise of the English Department as a separate entity, Phineas Nichols returned to the public schools of Portsmouth, New Hampshire. Mr. Adams, as had his predecessor, had held him in high regard, which he expressed years later in a letter to Mr. Cleaveland:

> I should in justice mention here the satisfaction I always derived from my intimate association with Mr. Phineas Nichols, first as Principal of the English school, and afterwards as my Assistant when the school had become united. The association then established between our families was a source of unmixed enjoyment at the time and of pleasant recollections since.

By December, 1846, Frederic Adams felt that he could remain no longer and submitted to the Board his letter of resignation.

This move apparently developed suddenly, yet in view of the reasons urged in the letter (which has unfortunately been lost), the Trustees, regretfully, felt "constrained" to accept the inevitable. They requested, however, that Mr. Adams remain for another term, and he acquiesced.

According to Nathan Withington, following Mr. Adams' departure a Mr. Holt, "a minister without a parish who lived in Byfield at the time," served as acting principal for part of a term. The Reverend Henry Durant, pastor of the Byfield Parish Church and a member of the Board of Trustees of the Academy, had first been elected "Teacher" but at the time (and understandably, as he was well aware of the predicament in which the school found itself) had declined. It appears from Ewell's *The Story of Byfield* that Mr. Durant was much beloved by his congregation, and it is likely that they did not wish to risk losing him. Nevertheless, when again asked to accept the position in August of the same year, he accepted, at the same time, however, retaining his pastorate.

Henry Durant, who died while holding office as Mayor of Oakland, California, was a remarkable man. Though this fact did not evidence itself strongly during his tenure at Dummer Academy, nor indeed during his residence in Byfield, a momentary digression to describe his career afterward seems justified.

At the time of the California Gold Rush thousands flocked West seeking prosperity overnight. The following quotation from the *Dictionary of American Biography* makes it clear why Henry Durant joined the mass migration:

> Among the many who were drawn to the West were
> a few earnest men who went in the interest of the welfare
> of their fellows. Henry Durant was one of this number.
> Awake to the possibilities of aiding in the educational
> development of the new state, he left . . . the East and
> arrived in California May 1, 1853.

Throughout the next few years Mr. Durant had but one goal in mind: to establish a college. Ten days after his arrival in the West he had gained support for the founding of an Academy in Oakland. In 1855 the academy was granted a charter as the College of California, and by 1860 an entering class had been prepared. When in 1868 this college became the University of California, Henry Durant was the logical choice to become her first President. Ill health forced his retirement after two years.

Recovering shortly, however, he was twice elected Mayor of Oakland.

In Byfield, though, the career of Henry Durant gave little sign of the great achievements to come. A graduate of Phillips Academy in Andover, and of Yale, he had been ordained pastor of the Byfield Parish Church late in 1833. In accordance with tradition, he soon occupied a place on the Board of Trustees of Dummer Academy and thus witnessed closely during the next fourteen years the diminishing fortunes of the school. During this time he lost his only daughter, the victim of scarlet fever at the age of eight years.

The sudden death of the little girl probably precipitated the illness of the parish minister which persisted for almost two years, often preventing the fulfilling of his pastoral duties. According to Gibbins Adams, a Byfield neighbor and former Dummer boy under Isaac Smith, some of the parish lost patience with Durant. This situation may have led to his dismissal from his charge in 1849, a few weeks before his resignation at the Academy.

In his *Centennial Discourse* Nehemiah Cleaveland expressed pain at having heard that Reverend Durant was not entirely successful or happy teaching at Dummer, adding only that "if intellect and scholarship, a refined taste and great amiability are all that a teacher needs, Mr. Durant should have made a 'capital' Preceptor." The Trustees' records reflect some difficulty, hinting at "certain evils encountered by him in his discipline and management of the scholars." Nathan Withington, who finished his preparation under Durant, suggests where part of the problem may have lain:

> Mr. Durant was a fine scholar, and an excellent teacher of pupils who were quick and anxious to learn, but quite the reverse with the stupid or careless. He seemed to me to be perfect until in after years I learned that my younger relatives looked back upon him with dislike approaching abhorrence.

Some interesting changes adopted into the bylaws during Henry Durant's stay may, by implication, give further indication of where the trouble lay. They required that "The Government shall, as far as practicable, be of a paternal character, appealing to the highest motives"; that "Corporal punishment must be known only as a last resort"; and that ". . . should a Trustee at any time be appointed Preceptor, his acceptance of such appointment shall be a virtual resignation of his office as Trustee. . ." Further, the boys in the school were more strictly limited to within Byfield Parish in their wanderings during their free time. Enlarged responsibility and power for the Prudential Committee was pre-scribed in careful detail. The duties of the Preceptor were, in fact, becoming little more than simply to teach.

In July of 1849 Mr. Durant resigned. On October 24, 1849, Gibbins Adams entered in his diary the following startling notice:

> . . . Revd Henry Durant and his Brother has [sic] taken the Factory and is about commencing a large business in the Manufactory of Furniture they are Calculating to employ 20 or 30 hands.

For a time the business thrived; then it, too, dwindled. A letter from Nehemiah Cleaveland to his friend Professor Packard at Bowdoin fills in the rest of the details:

> . . . During the last six years of my residence in By-field, the Rev. Henry Durant was my pastor . . . a man, withal, of more than common intellect—of sweet temper and gentle manners — you may easily see what a prize that was in such a place as Byfield. He went afterward into business and was unfortunate. I heard of him as still living in Byfield — overwhelmed with debt — despon-dent — if not despairing. I invited him to come to Brooklyn and see if we could not find something for him to do. He complied. I soon ascertained that he was very anxious to go to California. I had some doubts of its expediency — but there seemed to be nothing else. So I went to work — I soon raised enough money to enable him to go . . . During the last twenty years I have watched his California career with interest — I have sometimes felt a pleasure in thinking that I had been permitted thus indirectly to contribute something toward the advancement of education on the shores of the Pacific.

Today we who are interested in Governor Dummer Academy may also take pleasure in thinking that much of Henry Durant's experience in the administration of a school must have derived from his years as a Trustee and a Preceptor in Byfield; we may take particular pleasure, too, in realizing that the great and good Nehemiah played so significant a part in the guiding of the fortunes of his friend.

Following the departure of Mr. Durant, school was temporarily suspended in order to make "necessary repairs and improvements," and while attempts were made to procure a suitable Preceptor. During this time discouragement, or it may have been preoccupation with other matters, reduced attendance at Trustee meetings to the point that lack of sufficient numbers to constitute a quorum was not unusual. Indeed, a suggestion was made that non-attending members be asked to resign their memberships so that quorums might more easily be attained.

In the fall of 1850 the Reverend Ariel P. Chute, a native of Byfield and a graduate of Bowdoin and the Andover Theological Seminary, was elected Preceptor. Once again the Board had turned for leadership to a Dummer alumnus and former student of Mr. Cleaveland (and of Samuel Adams). Mr. Chute was experienced both as a preacher and teacher, having occupied a pulpit in South Lynnfield, Massachusetts, for six years, and at various times acting as principal at Warren Academy, Woburn, and Milton Academy in addition to Dummer. The sciences occupied the center of Mr. Chute's interest and, as Nehemiah suggests, undoubtedly played a significant role in the course of study during that gentleman's two year tenure at the Academy. It is known that he owned a valuable collection of minerals and that upon his departure from the school in 1852 this collection was purchased by the Trustees and so remained behind. For a time Mr. Chute returned to the ministry, but from 1861 he was in the civil service at the Custom House in Boston and then an assistant in the Boston office of the United States Treasury.

The years since Nehemiah Cleaveland's resignation had seen the school struggling to regain solid ground, having lost its footing as the result of an ill-starred experiment. The struggle had been bitter and was not yet won, but Dummer had doggedly clung to life and in the next six years was to take some firm steps forward.

CHAPTER VII

Henshaw, Albee, John S. Parsons, and Foster

WEST NEWBURY, July 14, 1858. . . . In later years the advantages of classical education having been extended to the inhabitants of every city and many towns, the number of scholars at "Old Dummer" has diminished until a few years since it was scarcely an institution. But the Trustees wisely held on to the fine farm left by Gov. Dummer, and a few years since they were fortunate enough to secure the services of Marshall Henshaw, M. A., as Preceptor. Under his able and fostering charge, "Old Dummer" is rising, phoenix-like, and parents are beginning to avail themselves of this rare opportunity for giving their sons a thorough course of study, in a healthy and charming locality, entirely free from contaminating influences. There is not even a candy-shop or a "depot" within two or three miles. A distinguished Essex County official, who was a scholar there some thirty years ago, could find nothing to invest pocket-money in but a pailfull of milk at a neighboring farmer's — his son, now a scholar, was fortunate enough to purchase a setting hen and a dozen duck's eggs, which were duly incubated.

So, in part, read a dispatch in *The Boston Journal* following Commencement Day in 1858. The writer was Samuel Perley, a student at Dummer under old Nehemiah; his father had studied under Abiel Abbot, and his grandfather had attended the Academy under Master Moody. The salubrious and retired setting of the Academy, "free from contaminating influences," is a familiar theme, running through descriptions of the school from the earliest days. (It is to be assumed that the absence of such worldly institutions as candy-shops and depots represented a recommendation more acceptable to the parents than the scholars.)

The tone of the dispatch is typical of all others that have come down from this period. The school under Marshall Henshaw, Preceptor since 1853, had been thriving. On the average, between thirty and forty boys had been in attendance each term for some years. The report of commencement proceedings for the previous year, too, serves to reflect this healthy condition in the Academy:

66

. . . The standard of the school as demonstrated by the examination is such as reflects distinguished honor upon the teacher. The thoroughness of the recitations not only exhibit industry on the part of the scholars, but constant and assiduous care in the preceptor; and more than this, the regard which every pupil bears him, shows a unity of interest and hearty cooperation which are the best marks of a good school.

Attendance at these "exhibitions," as the commencement exercises of the day were termed, was large. At both of those referred to, the fabled Enoch Boynton, who had studied seventy years earlier under Master Moody, was present on the platform. (The reader would find reward in an excursion into the realm of stories surrounding "Old Boynton." His eccentricities are but hinted at by pointing out that his two sons, one born while he was building a section onto his house, and one while a section was being razed, were given the middle names of *Adding* and *Tearing*). At the exhibition in 1858 John L. Ewell, later a professor of theology and author of *The Story of Byfield,* presented in Latin the salutatory address — "very neatly conceived," to quote the correspondent of the day. Years later in his book Professor Ewell quoted a Swedish proverb: "The teacher is the school." Then in glowing terms he proceeded to pay tribute to his old preceptor as a teacher of "eminent merit."

In his progress to Dummer Academy Marshall Henshaw had come a long way from the log cabin in Pennsylvania, his birthplace, "which the wolves howled about at night," according to Dr. Ewell. He had worked his way through Amherst and then through theological seminary. Before coming to Byfield, he had been Master of Hopkins Academy in Hadley, Massachusetts, and Pinkerton Academy in Derry, New Hampshire. Though he is said to have been somewhat stern in aspect, he was warm of heart. As a teacher he was thorough and demanding. The programs for the exhibitions stand as mute evidence of the classical emphasis of the instruction, and the recorded plaudits of those present on such occasions are witness to its effectiveness.

After almost seven years of gratifying success at the school, it must have come as a severe shock to the Board to receive Mr. Henshaw's resignation in September of 1859. Mr. Henshaw's decision to leave cannot be laid to neglect or lack of encouragement by the Board. This body was at the time led by its President for forty-two years (1852-1894), the Reverend John Pike of Rowley;

Mr. Asahel Huntington, prominent businessman and prosecuting attorney in Essex and Middlesex counties; and the by now renowned scholar and former Principal of the Boston Latin School, Benjamin Apthorp Gould. These men labored hard to so arrange school affairs as to provide its Master with assurance of security. At the Exhibition in 1859, shortly after the decease of Mr. Gould (a graduate of the Academy under Dr. Allen), the Preceptor and the Trustees alike expressed the deepest sense of loss. This good man, for years the leader of the most famous secondary school of classical learning in the country, had devoted a large part of his time, freely offering both of his means and his spirit to the strengthening of the Academy.

In hopes of providing a more regular income for the school, to supplement tuition, the Trustees in 1863 had begun investigation into the advisability of selling the Dummer farm and investing the proceeds. With the guidance of Mr. Huntington, they even petitioned the Supreme Judicial Court of Massachusetts for permission to do so if it seemed wise. At first defeated by a vote of the members in 1854, the move to promote the sale at a price of not less than $10,000 was finally adopted early in 1859.

Had the Board succeeded in its intention, it would undoubtedly have wrought immediate benefit to the Academy. Yet looking back from the perspective of 100 years, how unfortunate such an act would have been! Today one of the strengths of Governor Dummer Academy lies in its lovely and spacious, yet highly functional setting, reaching from the main campus across to Broadback Hill behind Ingham House, north to Whipple Field and the old Noyes farm, then across to the new Huggins Track and Field and Morse Field, and finally beyond the Turnpike to the Ould Newbury Golf Club, bordered by the salt marshes.

Mr. Henshaw's salary during most of his stay amounted to $600 cash, the use of the Commons for his family, and all of the tuition moneys, the total value amounting to well over one thousand dollars a year. Out of this, however, he had to provide fuel and pay an assistant up to $300. In 1858 tuition was raised to $10.00 a term ($3.75 to Byfield scholars).

It is unfortunate that the school was not to continue for many more years in the course which it had followed from 1853 to the summer of 1859. At least one alumnus of that period, George C. Hazelton, reminiscing decades later (in a letter published in *The Archon* for April, 1917), confirms the impression that the days were happy ones for those connected with the old Academy:

. . . It was when Marshall Henshaw was at the head of the institution . . . No better teacher ever graced a school in all New England. It was when sweet Madame Bailey, "widowed in her prime," kept the academy boarding house [the Mansion House], with "fun and food in plenty." It was when the neighboring girls were in their bloom, "and all went merry as a marriage bell."

However memory may have garlanded the charms of "sweet Madame Bailey" and the neighboring girls, one cannot doubt the affection which the writer felt for that day and place.

At the conclusion of the year 1859, however, the Trustees were obliged to ask Mr. Henshaw to take a reduction in salary. This he could not see fit to do. When invited before the Board to explain the reasons for his resignation, he ascribed them first to his isolated position, the distance from the church, the absence of a school for his young children, and the somewhat inferior quality of the scholars at the Academy. To these were added the reduction in his pay and an offer which he had received to join the faculty at Rutgers College. When Mr. Huntington asked him if he would stay if the Board could arrange to pay him more, he replied that he "should not want to decline the appointment in Rutgers College for an uncertainty after the present year."

Reluctantly the Trustees accepted his resignation and made plans to see what they could do about filling the vacancy. In their records for October, 1859, appears the following tribute to the man whose services they were losing:

Resolved — That we part with Mr. Henshaw as the principal of our Academy, with very great regret — as we have found him, on an experience of six years, to be a most faithful — conscientious — able & successful teacher & governor of the school, and especially an exact & most thorough *classical leader* — that we tender him our kind & respectful regards, as a man, and our best wishes for his future success and usefulness, in the higher & wider sphere of labor & duty, to which he is now called, and for the health & happiness of himself and family.

To this Mr. Henshaw replied in kind, expressing his friendship for the Trustees and his continuing interest in the school.

As her one hundredth birthday rapidly approached, it could not be denied that Dummer Academy had been blessed with the presence of a number of gifted and able Teachers : Marshall Henshaw and Nehemiah Cleaveland; Samuel Adams and Benjamin Allen, (who were likely, had their sojourns been longer, "to have proved most royally"); and, of course, the incomparable Master Moody. Yet in retrospect this blessing seems to have been, as well, her greatest bane. For in every instance the Teacher had been the school, and when the Teacher left, the school languished until it became necessary to begin again at the beginning.

As soon as Mr. Henshaw's resignation appeared inevitable, the Trust sought to procure the services of Benjamin Stanton, a Bowdoin graduate and at the time Principal of the Union College preparatory school. The negotiations failed, and with Mr. Henshaw's departure school was temporarily suspended pending appointment of a new principal. Meanwhile the Board pulled in its belt a notch and undertook a survey of its charge. More explicit conditions for leasing the farm, in case it should not sell, were laid down, including the injunction "that the tenant should attend church and help support the gospel." Brickwork on the Mansion House was cemented, and other necessary repairs made.

Early in 1861 the Academy reopened under the new Principal John S. Parsons, a teacher of experience. A year later, in July, the records report the satisfaction of the Trustees, following their examination of the twenty students then in attendance, "many of them young — & most of them new scholars." At this time decision was reached to set up for the following spring "appropriate observances of Prayer, Praise, and Public Discourse and all due Social Festivities . . . ," in observation of the centenary of Dummer Academy, and to call upon the Sons of Dummer to help in the preparations. By great good fortune Nehemiah Cleaveland was selected to be Orator of the Day. No happier contribution could have been made to posterity, for the meticulous groundwork done by this able scholar in putting together his discourse has provided us not only with a most interesting history of the first one hundred years of the school, but a collection of materials, as well, which lend authority to almost every word. Mr. Cleaveland wrote scores of letters to alumni and friends of the school in his search for facts. Many of the answers he saved; they are still available for reference.

In the fall of 1862, at the end of a year and a half in office, Mr. Parsons succumbed following a short illness. His unexpected death was another blow to the Trustees, for in his brief tenure he and his wife had gained the respect of all. For some months afterward

Mrs. Parsons, at the invitation of the Board, made her home at the Mansion House. (Her husband's successors and their families would have lived in Commons, known as "the Master's House.")

> . . . this Institution has lost a teacher of rare qualifications—of exact scholarship—of high ideas of discipline and order — and ambitious to make the School one of the first grade . . .

So wrote the Trustees in their records.

Mr. Solon Albee, formerly head of Pinkerton Academy, was elected Principal to succeed Mr. Parsons but, apparently disenchanted and dissatisfied, departed in little more than a year to take a position at Middlebury College. His successor, Edwin L. Foster, a graduate of Amherst College, remained but a few months, resigning in turn in November, 1864, because of bad health.

It is ironic that the Centennial celebration, looking back proudly over 100 years of achievement, should have come when it did, during the brief tenure of Mr. Albee, when the fortunes of Dummer Academy were at a low ebb, indeed. In the three brief principalships of John Parsons, Albee and Foster (lasting from April, 1860, to November, 1864), only thirty-two boys in all attended school, according to the 1884 *Catalogue of the Officers and Students of Dummer Academy*. Not in the least deterred by these facts, however, the remarkable Nehemiah Cleaveland, on the day of the Centennial, looked with confidence to the future of the Academy. "It has been running down for a good while," he wrote in the Appendix of his *Centennial Discourse,* "and it will take time and patience, as well as energy, judgment and prudence, to build it up again. Let it rest awhile . . ."

On August 13, 1863, the day following the Centennial celebration, the following lines headed the report of the affair in a Newburyport newspaper:

> The Dummer Centennial passed off yesterday under the most favorable auspices. The day was delightful, as fine as any, we will venture to say, that has shone on the school for the century that has elapsed since its foundation. At an early hour the roads leading from the various railroad stations — Newburyport, Byfield, and Rowley, were thronged with carriages and foot passengers, hastening to participate in the festivities of the day.

Let Nehemiah fill in the physical details:

> . . . The immense tent of the Essex Agricultural Society
> — kindly loaned for the occasion — covered a large part
> of the open space in front of the Mansion House grounds.
> Above and around it waved flags and streamers. Within,
> every arrangement that judgment and taste could devise,
> had been made both for convenience and effect. A
> broad and elevated platform occupied the eastern end.
> The large space in front was filled with comfortable
> settees. Conspicuous at the western end was the portrait
> of Governor Dummer . . .

The Newburyport correspondent, guided, one would guess, more
by enthusiasm than by reason, estimated an attendance of three
thousand people — alumni, friends, and neighbors of the school.
At any rate, the crowd just about filled the "settees" provided,
coming close, in all likelihood, to Mr. Cleaveland's figure of
1,000. Asahel Huntington, as secretary of the committee in
charge of arrangements, had corresponded widely "with all the
loyal States," for, of course, the nation was in the midst of the
Civil War, a fact which did not pass unnoticed during the day and
which sounded a solemn note in the midst of the festivities. 119
alumni actually signed their names in a book provided for the
purpose. The oldest of these, Jonathan Perley of Salem, had been
a student under Master Moody.

The program, beginning with the procession of Trustees, alumni,
and invited dignitaries, accompanied musically by the Rowley
band, included the rendition of a number of odes written especially
for the occasion, as well as numerous "eloquent remarks" by
various individuals of note. There was, as well, a dinner "in the
best style of Mr. Smith, the famous Boston caterer." But by far
the outstanding event of the day was the historical address by
Nehemiah Cleaveland, which occupied "two mortal hours," but
which "finely written and eloquently delivered . . . was listened to
with breathless and undivided attention." The reader, even today,
who dips into Nehemiah's *Discourse,* published according to the
unanimous vote of the alumni present at the occasion, is well
rewarded and entertained — and may be forgiven for regretting
that he was not present when the orator delivered it.

Such was the first Centennial day for Dummer Academy.
Though future prospects at the time seemed dim, it was not to be
the last.

NEHEMIAH CLEAVELAND

CHAPTER VIII

Stanton, Ebenezer Greenleaf Parsons, and Perkins

In a footnote to the printed edition of his *Centennial Discourse*, Nehemiah Cleaveland informs the reader of the resignation of Solon Albee and the appointment of Edgar L. Foster, of whom he says:

> . . . The present incumbent is quite a young man, — but time will be mending that fault every day. So far as I can learn he makes a very favorable impression. Let him work on in patience and in hope, and he cannot fail of success.

Conditions were indeed unstable at Dummer. Before the edition could be printed, it became necessary to add a "post-script" to the footnote:

> I have just heard that Mr. Foster has resigned and the school is again closed. My exhortation fails in this case — but I let it stand. It may do for the next man.

Nehemiah was a better prophet than he knew. On May 28, 1866, "Professor Stanton of Bates College," was elected the new Teacher, and in the next six years enjoyed considerable success.

It is certain that the new appointment pleased Nehemiah. Very likely he had had a hand in it, for he himself was elected a Trustee of the Academy at the very meeting during which the selection was made. Both Levi, the new Preceptor, and his brother Benjamin were graduates of Mr. Cleaveland's alma mater, Bowdoin College. It was Benjamin whom the Trustees had tried to bring to Byfield in 1859. Levi had taught at New Hampton Institute and been Principal at the high school in Newburyport before moving to the Maine State Seminary in Lewiston. When that institution grew into Bates College, Mr. Stanton became Professor of the Greek Language and Literature.

The Academy's enrollment was high and the school active under Mr. Stanton. In the winter term of 1867 sixty-two boys studied there. From term to term numbers ranged generally from forty to sixty. The popularity of this skilled teacher drew boys from throughout New England and beyond, as is witnessed by this testimony made years later by one of his students.

> I remember the day in March, 1867, when I landed at Dummer. Thirteen other young men came all the way from Maine, drawn by the reputation of the great and good teacher.

In six years almost two hundred boys came to the school, more than six times the total for the preceding half dozen years.

As one might guess from Levi Stanton's background, the course of study was largely classical. The normal program covered a three-year period, though younger boys could take a year longer:

> . . . The instruction is *thorough,* and based upon the principle that a man's education depends on the amount of *discipline* he has received, and not upon the *extent* and *variety* of subjects he has pursued. It is a primary object to induce the pupils to think and reason for themselves.

So asserts the catalogue for 1869. (The last sentence bears kinship to the philosophy held by Dr. Edward Eames, so widely respected as Headmaster of the Academy from 1930 to 1959.)

In addition to calling attention to familiar virtues — "The retirement of the place, and its freedom from stores. . .and other places of resort" — the catalogue calls special attention to the free Library of the school, and the "good set of Apparatus, adequate to illustrate all the important principles of Natural Philosophy and Chemistry. . .owned by the Sons of Dummer, and devoted to the use of the Institution." Attention was called to the newly organized Dummer Fraternity, a literary society ". . . conducted with much system and order." In its exercises were included such activities as declamations, discussions, and the reading of dissertations.

"He was an inspiring teacher," reported one alumnus to *The Archon* in 1907, speaking of Mr. Stanton. "He had a tact for bringing out the best there was in one."

There is no doubt of Mr. Cleaveland's disappointment upon the resignation of Stanton, due to ill health, in the spring of 1872. To Professor Packard he wrote:

> I have received notice of a meeting of the Trustees of Dummer Academy, to be held in reference to the

resignation of Mr. Stanton. I suppose that he has made up his mind to go — I conclude that an effort will be made to elect a Principal. Do you know where we can find a person who will be just the man for that place?

You know something about it. It is not so desirable as some other situations that can be named. But still, something can be said in its favor. As regards emolument — I think that for the last two years, it has been worth to Mr. Stanton, about $1,600 a year. A part of this came from the Academy fund — and the rest was tuition money. Mr. Stanton has been popular . . .

Mr. Cleaveland was well aware of the difficulties to be faced at Dummer, but he remained until his death a steadfast worker for the school.

Apparently, by the time of Levi Stanton's departure, the physical and financial conditions of the Academy were re-established on a sound basis. *The Newburyport Herald,* reporting upon commencement activities at the end of the preceding year, had given a favorable account not only of the academic excellence exhibited in the course of the program, but of circumstances in general:

. . . Dummer never looked better in its refined, classical and well shaded beauty than it did on this, the 107th [sic] anniversary of the Institution. The buildings have been kept in excellent repair, and the noble trees which surround it are in all their mature magnificence. . .The school seems to be in a prosperous condition. Through the judicious, efficient management of the Treasurer, E. S. Moseley, Esq., the funds of the Institution have been greatly increased.

Edward S. Moseley, son of Ebenezer Moseley of Newburyport (Trustee of Dummer from 1813 to 1839), served actively and constructively as a Trustee of the Academy for almost half a century, 1852 through 1900. A shipowner and merchant in the East India trade, later a banker and businessman, throughout his term of office he devoted himself usefully and generously to the interests of the school, sending three of his sons to study there. The Trustees' records confirm the relatively healthy financial condition of the Academy in this period. In fact, though nothing came of it, Treasurer Moseley felt that the time had arrived to add a new school building.

In the 'sixties and 'seventies the membership of the Board was undergoing considerable change. President Pike, blind from 1868, but continuing in energy and intelligence, Mr. Moseley and a few others spanned the period, but at least four valuable and long-term incumbents were lost. Colonel Jeremiah Colman, from one of Byfield's original families and a graduate of the Academy under Isaac Smith, was a faithful and practical-minded member of the Board for thirty-seven years (1829-1866). Colonel Daniel Adams, also a graduate under Isaac Smith, was a Trustee for thirty-eight years (1828-1866), for many of which he was a key member of the Farm Committee. A third graduate of Isaac Smith's day, long the keeper of a lively boarding house near the Academy, Captain Daniel Noyes served as a Trustee for thirty-one years and was a colleague of Colonel Adams on the Farm Committee. Asahel Huntington, whose term on the Trust extended from 1846 until his death in 1870, was the fourth severe loss to the Board. Beginning with Nehemiah Cleaveland in 1866, twelve new Trustees were elected in a ten-year span of time.

The Reverend Ebenezer Greenleaf Parsons, into whose hands the fortunes of Dummer Academy were placed in 1872, was an older man than it had been the custom of the Board to employ. Almost sixty years of age, he had for a total of thirty-two years served as a Congregational minister in the towns of Freeport, Maine, and Derry, New Hampshire, prior to taking over Pinkerton Academy a few years before. (This small New Hampshire academy must have felt a little as if it were a proving ground for Dummer Academy preceptors, for several had come straight to Byfield from there, and more were destined to do so.) For the next ten years the Academy was to adopt a character heretofore foreign to it, for by vote of the Trustees girls were admitted, at the full tuition charge. Mrs. Parsons, second wife of the new Principal and herself a teacher, became superintendent of the female portion of the student body.

The 1884 *Catalogue of Officers and Students of Dummer Academy* does not deign to list the girls who studied at the school, though there may have been as many as twenty in attendance during any single term. Carrie Knight Ambrose and Carrie S. Dummer were graduates of this period. Many of the girls, through an organization founded in 1910 and known as the Dummer Allies, remained for years amongst the most loyal supporters of the Academy. Certainly their presence in the school enlivened the atmosphere. One story is told of a day boy who, on his way to school, noticed that some workmen in a gravel pit had uncovered a nest of young snakes, "two or three quarts" of them. Collecting them in a can he brought them into the school room and placed them under the stove. The first inkling poor Mr. Parsons had of them came when the girls began to disperse in panic.

It is traditional that young girls despise snakes and that young boys take advantage of this aversion. Yet the young gentlemen of Dummer would countenance no real insult to their attractive classmates. On one occasion when Mrs. Ambrose, then Carrie Knight, was the sole girl in a mathematics class, the instructor, a young and callow assistant one would guess, held her up to ridicule for failing to solve a problem quickly. The score of boys in the class refused to continue the recitation until apology had been made to Miss Knight.

An attempt was made to continue emphasis on the classical program of study, but a course in English studies was reinstituted as well, with some flexibility between the two. In Mr. Parsons's ten years, over ninety boys graduated. For a while at the beginning, the general enrollment held up well. But the times were difficult. In the middle 'seventies the country found itself projected into a serious depression, following the turbulent Reconstruction period in the South. Enrollment declined. With money scarce, the expense of upkeep at the school ate into the Academy savings. Mr. Parsons in 1877 accepted a $200 cut in his salary. The Treasurer, Mr. Moseley, found it necessary to resign his office to concentrate on his extensive business interests. The school entered once again upon difficult days.

Then, on April 17, 1877, the Academy lost a great friend — and this *History* a benefactor. On that day death came quietly to Dr. Nehemiah Cleaveland, LL.D., whose warm concern for Dummer had extended from 1809, his student days under Isaac Smith, to the last hour of his life. As Preceptor for nineteen years and Trustee for eleven, he devoted himself unstintingly to fostering the wisest course for the school. From his first youthful observation of that "short, nice, rubicund, but kindly and scholarly-looking old gentleman," Isaac Smith, through his meticulous compilation of the history of the first one hundred years of the Academy, and down to his last observations upon the retirement of Levi Stanton, he has provided an invaluable fund of material and is due credit for much that may be of interest in this two-hundred year *History*. In continuing the book from here, this writer is acutely conscious of having lost a friend and guide, from whom he can only hope he has learned enough to proceed successfully alone.

Just one year before his death Nehemiah had been present at a "grand reunion of the alumni at Dummer Academy," in connection with the annual Exhibition. He had indulged in some reminiscences for the assembled company which, according to the report in the *Salem Gazette,* "included a tolerably full representation of the younger graduates, and a very fair representation of the older ones." One may read between the lines, however, that the school's following, as well as its enrollment, was reduced. One startling event in the course of these festivities occurred when the President of the Board, having just made feeling reference to some friends of the school who had recently passed away, requested that the Boxford Band (which otherwise "acquitted itself with great credit during the day") "respond with music befitting these sacred memories":

> . . . but that musical body having stepped outside, and not being in immediate hearing of the request, struck up, with comical effect, the lively air with which it was already prepared to close the formal festivities. But it expressed its good will toward the sentiments that had been uttered by playing the dirge afterwards as soon as the state of the case had been made known.

Such remarkably human failings as these — together with such ludicrous, but worrisome accidents as the drowning of one of Captain Knight's cows in the school's spring in 1879 — serve as assurances that this *History* will never take itself too seriously.

As was not unusual whenever the school showed some need for resuscitation, attendance at the Trustees' meetings now fell off seriously. Possibly crises at the Academy arose at those times when the Trustees had sufficient worries of their own elsewhere. At any rate, by 1881 the situation had become serious enough for a quorum of the Board to adopt a resolution that any member who had without explanation failed to attend meetings for two years, ". . .and who shall have neglected to perform the duties to which he may have been appointed . . . shall be deemed to have resigned." On November 7, 1881, a special meeting was held to discuss the state of the Academy. President Pike had in hand a letter of resignation from Mr. Parsons which, after some general discussion, was offered and accepted. The following resolution was read into the minutes:

> — That we recognize the faithfulness and ability of Mr. Parsons in discharging the duties which have devolved

upon him, as Preceptor of Dummer Academy, the earnestness with which he has striven to secure scholars, under circumstances of the greatest difficulty, the efforts he has made to advance their intelligence and guard their morals, and the care he has taken to preserve and improve that portion of our estate which was allotted for his support; and we also testify to the readiness of his accomplished wife to assist him in his labors. . .

From all indications, Mr. Parsons had been a competent teacher, but it was apparent that, almost seventy years of age, he was not the one to lead the school out of its new difficulties.

*   *   *   *   *

On June 19, 1888, Dummer Academy attained another significant milestone: her 125th anniversary. As orator of the day, William Dummer Northend, alumnus (Class of 1830) and Vice-President of the Trustees, took due notice in his historical address of this achievement. The notable events of the preceding six years, however, are best reflected in the after-dinner remarks of Headmaster John Wright Perkins, successor to Mr. Parsons:

It is safe to say that in no previous period of the same length has the school undergone so many changes in buildings and conveniences, as during the past six years. When the school was reorganized six years ago, it entered upon what many were pleased to call "a new departure." This, however, is a form of words which is often inappropriately applied and misleading; as, in the present case, the change was an attempt to return to first principles. This school was founded as a boys' classical school. It was a boarding school, a home school, and the nucleus of the school has been of this character during a considerable portion of its existence. But the same name often has different meanings at different periods; and a boys' boarding school suggests very different provisions now from what it did a hundred or even fifty years ago.

The time when twenty or more boys in addition to the master's family could be stowed away in the Mansion House, with any degree of satisfaction to parents or pupils, has very decidedly long passed. This was very manifest during the first year of the present administration. Accordingly at the end of the first year, the addition was made to the master's house [Commons] whereby the present convenient culinary accommodations were obtained — a very important acquisition, by the way, for a school like this — several additional rooms for boys and other much needed conveniences. Another two years gave us the new dormitory, last summer the new gymnasium building and last fall much needed repairs and improvements in the Academy building. . .

But what about the school, its patronage and its work? During these six years we have had one hundred and thirty-five different pupils. They came from sixteen different states and three foreign countries. . .

Many have attended with no intention of continuing their school training beyond the curriculum of the Academy; yet a large proportion of the students have gone from here to colleges or to scientific schools. The work we have attempted to do is somewhat unique. We have endeavored to take boys at almost any stage of advancement and set them at work and give them help at the point most for their advancement, without insisting upon rigid classification. Of course, such an attempt honestly carried out, requires a large force of instructors in proportion to the number of pupils. Thus during the year just closed with an average of about thirty pupils, four experienced teachers have been regularly engaged in actual teaching for at least six hours a day, and for myself, I doubt whether in my experience of more than twenty years as a teacher, I have ever spent more hours in teaching than during the past year, with this small number of pupils and so many assistants. . .

The year just past has been one of as good work, I think, as any that we have had and one of very little friction in matters of discipline. Five young men go out from us fitted for college and two for the scientific course at Cornell University. . .

The "new departure" in 1882 had begun with the Board's retaining of John W. Perkins to head the school. A graduate of Harvard in 1865, recipient of an A. M. degree from the same university in 1871, Mr. Perkins had since 1868 been the highly successful Principal of the Salem, Massachusetts, High School. The respect in which he was held in that community is reflected

DUMMER ACADEMY (CIRCA 1884):
The Mansion House, Commons, and Parsons Schoolhouse

in newspaper accounts such as that appearing in the *Salem Register* at the end of his first year at the Academy:

> It was a serious loss to Salem when Mr. Perkins left our High School, but his going to Dummer has proved of incalculable benefit to that school. . .Parents can now send their boys to Dummer Academy with the fullest confidence that they will receive the best attention, morally and physically as well as intellectually.

As part of the new arrangement, Mr. Perkins took full responsibility for the Academy farm and the general care of the school buildings. The sole obligation of the Board was to see that all was kept up and managed according to agreement. Having taken all of the reins into his own hands, the new Headmaster instituted the "return to first principles." Since the Academy was to resume its historical role as primarily a "home" school, with many of the boys living on the premises under the "immediate care" of the Principal, girls were no longer admitted. Tuition was set at $75.00 per year, the same as at Exeter and Andover, and at one-third of that amount for qualified Town of Newbury scholars. The academic program focused largely on classical studies.

From the first the arrangement was a success. On December 14, 1882, a committee of Trustees reported to the full body that the system "has been largely appreciated" and ". . .it is evident that with the increase in pupils in the future that [sic] the subject of additional rooms will become an important one."

The Trustees, the Sons of Dummer, and Mr. Perkins himself provided sufficient funds at the end of the first year for the enlarging of boarding and dining facilities at the Commons, the Principal's house. Repairs were made to the Mansion House, where the boarders were under the supervision of one of the faculty assistants. From friends of the school, small gifts to permit further improvements to the plant were forthcoming — even including, from one, two cows, valued at sixty dollars. The financial condition of the Academy was not strong, but the promise of better days apparently warranted such expenditures as could be managed.

The earliest copies of *The Archon*, which began publication in 1884, show that spirits at the school were high. The football team enjoyed its first season, under the captaincy of rugged, handsome John Hamilton Morse, who was later to play several important roles in the destiny of his school and whose name today is attached to the principal athletic field at Governor Dummer.

Also in 1884, for the first time, a telephone was installed at the Academy. Mr. Northend earned the gratitude of his colleagues on the Board (as well as of succeeding generations) by performing a Herculean service in compiling the *Catalogue of the Officers and Students of Dummer Academy* (1763-1884), to this day an invaluable reference.

The construction of the new dormitory (the new building was to be destroyed by fire a short ten years later) eased the boarding situation. Designed by Mr. Northend's son, also an alumnus of the school, it was dedicated in October, 1885. Once again the finances of the Academy had been stretched to the maximum. The report of the Building Committee tells the story:

> By begging some, borrowing some, and with the help of Master Perkins, who has expended from his own means for the purpose, they [the Trustees] have hitherto been able to accommodate the steadily increasing numbers who applied for admission, without material risk to the principal fund, and at the opportune moment, when it seemed they could not further meet the increasing demands for room, the income from the legacy of Mrs. Sarah Hale Stickney of Lowell [$10,000], given in memorial of her father, a former trustee, became available, and by relieving the other funds, rendered it possible to erect this new dormitory, without too much reducing the funds devoted to the support of instruction.

The Perkinses' devotion to the strengthening of the Academy is evident throughout the records of the day. Mrs. Perkins not only assisted her husband materially with the care and supervision of the boarding students, but she is largely credited as the moving force behind the building of the new gymnasium in 1887. In the records of the Board appears a vote "that the thanks of the Trustees be given to Mrs. Perkins for her arduous and energetic labors in securing funds and in the erection of the Gymnasium." Thirty-eight years later Master Perkins and his wife returned once more to the Academy on the occasion of the renaming, in their honor, of this same building, newly removed to another location. To the fund for its reconditioning and redecoration, Perkins boys from as far-distant places as Japan had contributed generously.

Despite the hopes, the efforts, and the successes, the situation of the Academy remained precarious. It may be that in taking on full responsibilities for all phases of the running of the institution, Mr. Perkins had overextended himself. At any rate, the concern of the Board shows more and more clearly in their records during the early 'nineties. Slowly the Trustees began to reclaim direct authority for supervision. In 1894 Mr. and Mrs. Perkins left Dummer Academy and returned to Salem, where he assumed the position of Superintendent of Schools. In the same year Mr. Northend became President of the Trustees in place of the Reverend Pike, who had performed in that office diligently for forty-two years. A year later the old minister resigned from the Board after over half a century of membership. Just previously the loss of two other long-term members had been sustained: the Reverend Samuel J. Spalding after thirty-five years and Dr. Benjamin Gould after more than thirty-four.

It was two more years before the Board could muster its forces for another concerted effort to re-establish the school on a firm footing. In the interim the Headmaster was the Reverend George B. Rogers, A. M., about whom little can be said except that he undertook his responsibilities faithfully. Described in the school catalogue as a man ". . .who has had experience as an instructor of boys both in college and in private schools," he focused his own teaching upon the classics. At the conclusion of one year, his contract was continued through another. After extended deliberation, but before the second year had ended, the Board voted to terminate the arrangement.

CHAPTER IX

Perley Leonard Horne

". . .the Academy has more than a history and an exceptionally attractive site; it has at the present time an
excellent and efficient staff of teachers, whose work
challenges comparison with the best work done in the
best schools of our country."

So, in part, read the 1898 report of a Harvard University
examining committee to the Board of Trustees of Dummer Academy. Master Perley Leonard Horne had controlled the destinies
of Dummer Academy from the fall of 1896, shortly after
the departure of the Reverend Rogers. Mr. Horne, an M.A. from
Harvard, was an energetic and purposeful leader soundly grounded
in education, with equally sound views toward the efficient
administering of a school which, though venerable, had passed
through difficult times. With four able assistants, he headed
Dummer Academy at the outset of a century which has seen the
school attain to a prestige unsurpassed in its history.

The indications are that Master Horne was before his time,
for although he clearly envisioned, indeed wrote down, what the
school might well become, he was unable to give it permanent
headway in this direction. He saw how the foundation should be
laid, but was unable to accomplish the laying of it. Nevertheless,
the period from 1896 to 1904 stands at the beginning of the
century as a brave prophecy of promise. It was this promise
which the examining committee from Harvard University recognized and praised warmly in their report to the Trustees.

If in 1898 the program of the school was of high quality, where
lay the Academy's weakness? This, too, appears in the report
of the investigating committee. The Mansion House (circa 1715)
was in lamentable condition, lacking in adequate sanitary facilities
and proper heating. Indeed, the Master and his family crowded into
Commons (circa 1836) with the boarders. At the moment there
is no clear evidence as to how the Mansion House was used,
except to accommodate a small public primary school for the
town of Newbury. Library facilities and equipment for the
science classes in Parsons Schoolhouse (1820) were inadequate,

84

as was the equipment in the gymnasium (now Perkins Dormitory — then since 1887 the newest building on campus). All of the buildings were sorely in need of paint.

There is ample evidence that parents who otherwise might happily have sent their children to school here, where superior instruction and unusual individual attention were available, were repelled by the bareness of the Academy plant. An item in the *Dummer News* for the fall of '98 comments on how pleasant it was ". . . to be able to sit under the shade of the widespreading trees that surround our school and enjoy the fresh sea breeze these hot Autumn days," for classes were held outside in good weather. The prospect inside must have been much less prepossessing.

The life of the school was animated, however. In Mr. Horne's first autumn the enrollment of boys was twenty, about eight of whom were boarders, the others coming from the vicinity. By 1901 the enrollment included forty-six boys, about half of whom were boarders, as well as twenty-one girls from the vicinity, who were permitted to attend the Academy as day students. In the spring of 1904, Mr. Horne's last months at the school, there were fifty boys, though girls were apparently no longer admitted.

In 1898, for a faculty of five, there were 150 recitations a week, an average of six classes a day per instructor. The unusually wide selection of courses included various classes in Latin, Greek, French, German, physics and chemistry, mathematics, English and daily themes (the latter required of all students), history, advanced mathematics, and natural sciences. Latin and math occupied the most time, with English and sciences not far behind. Graduates under Mr. Horne were already at Harvard, MIT, Boston University and Columbia. The class day ran from 9:00 A.M. until 3:00 P.M., with an hour out for lunch and an hour and a half of supervised study from 7.30 until 9:00 in the evening. With the one exception that the bed hour was set at 9:30, forty-five minutes earlier than today, the daily schedule was similar to what it is now.

The academic program was a challenging one and in certain striking ways anticipated aims being widely encouraged today. Provision for individualization of instruction was emphasized. The catalogue pointed out that while the school prepared pupils for entrance to college, yet it offered ". . . an exceptionally complete course for those who have no further study in view. The needs of the individual are consulted with an aim to develop the best in him." The course of studies bears out this claim. In addition to the Preparatory Course for younger boys, the offerings included complete programs for students interested in majoring in Classics, the Sciences, or English.

A most interesting aspect of the program was the requirement that all students in the school write a daily theme. These were to be short (they ranged from forty to about 200 words in length), could be on any subject, and had as their chief purpose "to teach fluent and correct expression." Daily consultations were held, and representative papers appeared regularly as a most entertaining feature of the *Dummer News.*

> . . . Each of us has to hand one theme in every day. We are allowed to choose our own subjects, which is pretty much like having to pick apples every day and being allowed to take from any trees in the orchard — very well until the whole crop is gone and you have to wait for more to grow.

So comments one student in the *Dummer News* — and one must grant that the program had nurtured a certain eloquence in the case of this writer.

I cannot resist quoting a very few of the themes, for they carry with them a vitality which brings to life the Dummer Academy of the period. The familiar shoreline at Plum Island might have been the inspiration for the first.

> The day was calm and still, and the surf broke in long regular breakers; so even and perfect were they that one could see for an instant a long chasm under the breaking wave. After the break a rush of snowy white foam would steal up the beach and quickly recede, leaving the little sand hoppers jumping about in great glee after their ducking.

This next, written by a young lady of the "Annex" (as the boys called the feminine portion of the student body), seems almost insignificant at first glance, as if the writer had run dry of ideas; but if the ability to express oneself easily and correctly was the aim of the program, then this description seems a notable success.

> One dark evening we watched the lightning when we could not hear the thunder very distinctly. I think I

never saw lightning so strange before. The sky looked as as if it were cracked all over, with light shining through the cracks.

Finally, boys in 1897 were, after all, boys!

> It falls nearly to her slender waist in a thick, light brown braid. It is not of the straight wiry sort that very long hair usually is, but it is wavy and fine like corn silk, with the sheen of corn silk in it. About her neck are little clinging curls. Down over her forehead it has a very charming to me, but troublesome to Emily, way of doing just as it pleases.

Such activities as the Byfield Church Socials and the annual Athletic Association barbecue played a lively part in the life of the school and are reported with enthusiasm in the school paper. The Dancing Class (apparently elective) was a more formal activity. The gymnasium, lighted by kerosene lamps and properly festooned each Thursday night, was the site of the class.

"Over in the corner by the red-hot stove stand the girls, casting timid glances at some foolish young men who are commenting on each others shoes," reports the *Dummer News*. Then the teacher calls for everybody to take a partner for the two-step.

> . . .After some modest hesitation a coat sleeve encircles a slender waist and the couples glide away into the darkest part of the gym, only to reappear whispering hurried words, which seem a part of the music. If anyone can judge by the number of melted collars or the amount of dust raised, I think they would say we have a pretty good time.

On the occasion of an actual dance, it was reported that ". . . but one thing marred what would otherwise have been a perfect evening. Our best dancers were room-bound." Being room-bound was the penalty for misdemeanors ranging from being late to breakfast to flunking a course. It consisted of being confined to one's room without company, when not at class or at meals — and of having to sit in the first row at chapel!

Team sports were the most popular form of exercise. At various times there were teams in football, lacrosse, "ice polo," basketball (a relatively new game), baseball, and track. The following interesting testimony to the rigors of the latter sport is recorded. In a track meet held in the Newburyport City Hall, Phelps of

Dummer, leading in the half mile ". . . was pushed in such a manner that he plunged forward and fell, striking his head violently against the steam pipes. . ." Practice for track was held around the trotting track at Fatherland Farm.

The first basketball game was played against Amesbury in 1902. Dummer failed to score in the first half, but returned "with surprising vivacity and not only held their opponents at bay, but succeeded in scoring seven points" — only to lose, I presume! Also worth quoting is this interesting report of a baseball game. It reads in its entirety:

> Our next game was at Haverhill. We lost a loosely played game. The score was 24 to 15. Haverhill made 17 errors.

Two years later the graduation issue of the paper records the fact that faculty member and coach Frank Moody, who played in the outfield, won the batting title by hitting .514, one point above the third baseman, who was a student!

Indeed, it was customary throughout Mr. Horne's regime for faculty members to play on the Academy teams. One picture of the football team shows Mr. Horne himself playing left tackle, with William Dudley Sprague (Master of the Academy from 1904-1906) stationed at quarterback in what looks very much like the T formation! Two other faculty members may be seen in the lineup. Of Mr. Horne's line play the *Dummer News* reports: "He was especially strong in opening holes in offense, but was less efficient on defense." The practice of playing teachers on teams later led to unpleasant relations with certain opponents and was eventually discontinued.

Though long before the days of the Ould Newbury Club, golf, too, was an interest. In 1900 a club of faculty and boys was formed and the "Quascacunquen" course laid out. This course was planned in a semicircle, traveling in a zig-zag fashion northwest from Sunset Rock over "stubble, swamps, mud, briars, stone walls, trees, brooks, telephone wires, barbed wires, and woodchuck holes."

> The boys have . . . laid out a links, lost innumerable balls, broken four or five clubs and all kinds of records . . . However, if they never do anything worse than hit a ball and then chase it, and can keep from using male golf language they will all go to Harvard.

THE ELECTRIC RAILWAY SWITCH NEAR THE MILESTONE

DUMMER ACADEMY'S FOOTBALL TEAM (CIRCA 1900):
Mr. Horne is at left tackle; Mr. Sprague behind center.

From the first tee the players must have had an impressive view of the Georgetown, Rowley, and Ipswich electric railway, which switched by the Milestone just below them. This long-awaited service was started in 1900. Cars left the Academy every half hour for Ipswich, Georgetown, and Newburyport. (One popular feature of the innovation was that it brought to the Academy dances young ladies from as far as Rowley and Haverhill.)

By 1898 Perley Horne was optimistic about the prospects of the Academy if the Trustees could see fit to devote sufficient funds to refurbishing the school plant. In his statement to the Board he outlined his working philosophy:

> . . . Our courses of study are arranged to meet the most advanced college requirements. With five teachers and thirty pupils, we give much individual instruction. Each teacher knows each pupil under him intimately . . . We encourage athletics but are not ruled by them . . . We have taken up many lines of athletic sport and have had our full share of success. The competition has been sharp, but manly. The teams that have represented the school have established a reputation for pure athletics. We intend to work daily toward our ideals in all our work and play."

The Board, to confirm their impression established by the confidence of the Master, requested the opinion of an examining committee from Harvard; upon receipt of a favorable report, they expressed their approval of Mr. Horne's plans by presenting him with a five-year contract. Plans were set into motion to restore the Mansion House for occupancy by the Master, as well as to make necessary repairs to other buildings. Mr. John Peirce, an alumnus and a member of the Board, contributed a gift to finance the building of a new dormitory, to be completed in 1903.

By 1902, however, the school had not prospered. Though some physical improvements had been made and the enrollment had shown a general increase, the Trustees were either unable or unwilling to underwrite further the Master's program for maintaining and improving gains. Mr. Horne had by this time sunk $5,000 of his own money in the school and faced the future with misgivings unless the Board were willing to commit itself.

An attempt was made to rescue the situation. Mr. Horne was persuaded to remain for two more years. More funds were sought. When in February, 1904, however, the Master put before the

Trustees his requirements for the ensuing year, it was the Board's turn to feel misgivings. A conditional agreement was reached — and finally withdrawn. Although much that Mr. Horne had recommended was to be accomplished in the years to follow, the time was not yet. The parting was on amicable terms. The man who had for eight interesting years been the head of the Academy, removed, with the recommendation of Harvard University, to Honolulu, Hawaii, to become Preceptor of a school there.

Paradoxically, in spite of her temporary set-back, Dummer Academy had moved closer to resurgence as a leader among the private secondary schools in New England.

CHAPTER X

Sprague, Ryther, and Ingham

When it became clear that he was leaving the Academy, Mr. Horne recommended to the Board that they consider appointing as his successor William Dudley Sprague. Mr. Sprague, an 1894 graduate of Harvard University (and, interestingly enough, a direct descendant of the Dudley family of which Governor Dummer's wife, Catherine, was a member), had accompanied Perley Horne to Dummer in 1896 and remained as his chief assistant until 1902. Then for a time he had moved into public school teaching in Salem, Massachusetts.

Athletic and energetic, Mr. Sprague had been popular with the boys, a man who shone in both physical and academic pursuits. He knew the school well and was familiar with the type of program carried on by his predecessor. He was accepted by the Board as an excellent answer to their needs. William Sprague's association with the school, in one capacity or another and at one time or another, extended as late as 1944. It was a pleasant one, based on mutual respect. The new Headmaster was handicapped at the start, however. He knew what his friend Perley Horne had wanted to do; he knew that when he had failed of accomplishing it, he had had to leave. Now Sprague was faced with trying to maintain what gains had been made, without the prospect of being able to carry them further in the direction in which they had been headed. It is a difficult task to try merely to maintain the status quo.

It appears that Mr. Sprague tried earnestly to carry on according to the limitations set down by the Board. The operating funds of the Academy were once again at a low ebb. New tuition rates were set, ranging as high as $600 per year for one boy living in a double room. A "canvasser" was hired to take charge of finding new students. Two years of relatively stand-pat administration began.

As part of the refurbishing of the school plant during the headmastership of Perley Horne, the Mansion House had been completely renovated and Peirce Cottage had been built (though apparently not completely finished until the spring of 1905). The

91

Schoolhouse, however, remained pretty much as it had been for some time, in relatively battered condition. This was the same building opened eighty-five years before, in April, 1820. In the spring of 1905, however, the Academy was the recipient of an unexpected gift. Mrs. Susan E. B. Forbes of Fatherland Farm gave $5,000 "for the improvement of the School House," in memory of her great grandfather, the Reverend Moses Parsons, friend and pastor of Lieutenant Governor Dummer, and the man who had presided when the doors of the Little Red Schoolhouse had first opened under Master Moody.

The Reverend Herbert E. Lombard, current pastor of the Byfield Parish Church, a friend of Mrs. Forbes, and a member of the Board of Trustees of the Academy (as well as an instructor in English for a time during Mr. Sprague's administration), took charge of arrangements and carried them through expertly. Donors were found to help furnish and equip the classrooms. One of them, Miss Emily Malbone Morgan, furnished the library, to be named at her request "the Judge Byfield Library of Dummer Academy" in honor of her ancestor for whom the parish was named.

Miss Morgan had for some years been a friend of the school, and as the representative of the religious society known as Companions of the Holy Cross had, since early in the decade, leased the farmhouse and the Red Schoolhouse from the Academy, instituting the Adelynrood retreat. In the spring of 1905, Miss Morgan renewed her lease on these buildings for five more years. Some years later, when the Academy had grown to need all of its facilities, Miss Morgan purchased property just to the north on Elm Street and established the present Adelynrood. Relations between the Academy and the Companions of the Holy Cross, a Protestant Episcopal society, have from the beginning been most cordial.

The new schoolhouse was to be comprised of the existing building, but moved onto new foundations and entirely redesigned. Decision was made to remove the structure to ". . . a point south of the road running into the Academy grounds from the Rowley Road to the Commons, and about ⅔ of the distance from the entrance of the grounds to the Commons," that is, from its location on the lawn in front of the Mansion House to its present position.

Through the earnest efforts of Mr. Lombard, much of the

additional money needed to complete the work satisfactorily was raised from friends of the school. Amidst stormy weather on Commencement Day, June 13, 1905, the cornerstone of the "new" Parsons Schoolhouse was laid. It was said to be ". . . the same stone that was under the second (1785) and third (1820) buildings . . . " The first year of Mr. Sprague's principalship thus ended on a happy note. Six boys constituted the graduating class on that Commencement Day, five of whom were planning to go on to college.

In January of 1906 the Trustees voted to offer Mr. Sprague a contract for a third year. This reappointment was reconsidered and rescinded in April. At the annual meeting in June, the following letter of resignation from the Master was read into the records:

> I wish to resign my position as Master of Dummer Academy and request that I be relieved of my duties at the close of the school year. I take this opportunity to thank each member of the Board of Trustees for every kindness which I have received from his hands and to say that I shall be pleased to be of any service in the transmission of my office.

Mr. Sprague returned to public school work, where he built a distinguished record which included twenty-four years as Principal of the Melrose, Massachusetts, High School. Years later, following his retirement from public education, he was to rejoin the faculty at Governor Dummer for a brief time.

1906-1907 was a turbulent year at Dummer. Master of the Academy was a young bachelor, Leon E. Ryther, who had previously taught for one year under Mr. Sprague. A graduate of the University of Maine, Ryther was an active, ambitious teacher, immensely popular with the boys and their parents. During his one year in charge of the Academy the enrollment climbed steadily, until in the spring there were fifty students, including thirty-five boarders. A debating society was started; a glee club was organized. In place of *The Dummer News,* which had earlier been discontinued, *The Archon* (using the title of the student publication which had flourished briefly in the 'eighties) was published.

The graduation issue of *The Archon,* dedicated to Mr. Ryther "in loving appreciation of his wise guidance and inspiring influence," lists nine graduates, eight of them going on to college. One of the students brought to Dummer by the new Master (and apparently taken with him when he left) was Booker T. Washington, Jr., son of the eminent negro President of Tuskegee Institute, who was author of *Up From Slavery*. While at the Academy young Booker was a dangerous threat at left halfback on the football team and stalwart catcher on the baseball team.

The aggressiveness of Master Ryther's nature was nowhere better illustrated than under the stress of the frightening and tragic accident in Commons on January 27, 1907, described the next day in the *Newburyport Daily News:*

> Frozen water pipes caused one of the worst disasters that has ever occurred at Dummer Academy, yesterday morning, when the boiler in the laundry at Commons House exploded with tremendous force, injuring the matron, Miss Clara Dawson, of Boston, so that it was necessary to amputate her right leg, and a piece of the flying iron struck Miss Martha Anderson, a young colored domestic, just below the right knee, almost severing that member.

A few steps away in the next room at the time of the explosion, Mr. Ryther carried the two painfully injured women to safety and assigned others of the staff to care for their wounds and to send for assistance. Mustering some of the boys, he then supervised the extinguishing of the fire which had immediately followed the blast.

Medical assistance from Newburyport and Haverhill was rushed on commandeered streetcars. It was determined that amputations were immediately in order. The boys were sent into Newburyport by street railway, while Commons dining hall was turned into an emergency operating room.

Early in the spring rumors began that Mr. Ryther was being asked to leave at the end of the year because he was not married, the Trustees desiring a married Master in order that his wife might act as Matron. The issue became a cause célèbre in the press of neighboring cities and towns; both the Academy and Mr. Ryther were the objects of considerable publicity. One newspaperman reported that the Master himself thought that he was being asked to leave because he was not well enough known as a school man. *The Newburyport Daily News* added the following comment on April 22, 1907:

> It is believed that the successor of Mr. Ryther as Master will be a Harvard man, and that in the future the

academy will be a fitting school for the university at Cambridge. The Masters of Dummer for a series of years have been Harvard men with the one exception of the retiring instructor.

In fact, however, the Trustees had met early in April and agreed to offer the Master a new contract for one year. This was explained by Fred M. Ambrose, for the Trustees, in a letter to the *News* in May. What had apparently happened was that in view of the success and enthusiasm accompanying his first year in charge, Mr. Ryther was emboldened to require of the Trustees a three year contract, not only for himself, but for the four members of his staff as well — and at larger salaries. The Board was willing to continue the contracts for another year, but, particularly in view of the recent unsuccessful five-year contract with Mr. Horne, would do no more. Since an agreement could not be reached, Mr. Ryther was asked to resign. Already, however, the publicity had brought him an offer to go as Principal to the Concord Academy. His whole staff resigned with him, including the Corresponding Secretary, or "canvasser," whom he took along to his new location.

Mr. Ambrose had ended his letter to the paper with the following attempt to set the record straight:

> Any man even from the smallest college in the country, is eligible for the position as Master at the Academy, and a graduate of Harvard will have no preference over any other candidate. It is the aim of the Trustees to secure the best talent that can be had and to make Dummer as good a preparatory school as there is in the country.

The Trustees were as good as their word; the new Master proved to be a Yale man!

At the annual meeting in June of 1907, Fred M. Ambrose was elected the new President of the Board; Mr. John Peirce of New York, donor of Peirce Cottage, was made Vice-President. At the same meeting announcement was made of the appointment of Dr. Charles S. Ingham (Yale, 1891; Ph.D. 1896) to head the Academy. The arrangements included a salary of $1,800 a year; the Mansion House, lighted and heated; and board for his family (including a young daughter, Katharine, and a young son, Travis) at Commons at cost. The new Master was willing immediately to roll up his sleeves and confront the problems that awaited him; he did not lack for confidence in his ability to cope with them. It was reported to the Trustees, upon announcement of his appointment, that he had said, "his price is $2,000 and when he proves the man for the place he looks for that in the near future." The Trustees were heartened and through their committee replied ". . . that we expected him to share in our prosperity. . ." A dozen years later Dr. Ingham was earning almost three times his original salary. His selection by the Board proved to be a most fortunate one for all concerned.

From the first the new head of the school set his sights, not on expanding the Academy into a large preparatory school of the nature of Exeter and Andover, but on building it into an effective small home school where the program could be kept flexible enough to meet the needs of a variety of individuals:

> It is the endeavor of this school to discover the possibilities of each student and to so train him that he may realize these possibilities if he will; to lead him to assume his proper responsibilities, to render service and to seek happiness in establishing and maintaining right relations with his environment.

So begins the catalogue at the start of Dr. Ingham's second year at the school.

The effort was not only to provide proper training for the typical preparatory school student, but to make provision, as well, both for older youths ambitious enough to make up work and finish the course in a shorter time than customary, and for youngsters who mature more slowly and need more time.

Charles Ingham was a vigorous man of forty years of age when he came to Dummer; in addition, he was a seasoned teacher and administrator. Following five years of graduate study both in this country and abroad, he had taught in three different private schools and at Yale, been Master of a school for boys in Washington, D. C., and assistant principal of Marston's University School in Baltimore, Maryland. In his address at the dedication of Ingham House in 1947, he indulged in reminiscence concerning his unpromising introduction to the Academy:

> I attended my first Commencement here forty years ago next week. It was a beautiful June day; nearly fifty good-looking young men were about the place, ten of whom received their diplomas that day. A half a dozen masters were on hand. One or two I approached, suggest-

ing their going on with me and the school. They did not care to do so and said so.

The break between the Ryther administration and the new one was clean and complete.

I went away, returning a month later . . . The grass was long and unkempt upon the campus. The boys were gone — not to return . . . Most doors were locked and the untagged keys thrown into a bucket for my use and contemplation.

"As I am dealing in gloom," continued the former Headmaster, "I may as well go on a bit further into my first year. We opened with thirteen boarding students and scarlet fever. When it was really cold the tank in the attic of the Mansion House suddenly dumped its tons of water, converting the kitchen into a skating rink." It is a pity that the rest of Dr. Ingham's speech cannot be quoted here, for it is full of interesting recollections and flashes of humor. Among the most interesting comments are those in which he expresses his gratitude to many of the friends of the school who helped overcome some of the major obstacles encountered during his twenty-three years incumbency: people like President of the Board Fred Ambrose; Mr. Edward P. and Miss Marion Noyes, neighbors of the Academy (Edward Parish Noyes was an active Trustee); Judge Cabot, Treasurer of the Board; the Reverend Mr. Lombard; Joseph N. Dummer and Ben Pearson, neighbors of the school and members of the Trust; John Hamilton Morse, the donor of Morse Field; Judge Alden P. White; Glenn Tilley Morse and James Duncan Phillips, of whom more later.

The Board was quick to recognize Dr. Ingham's value to the Academy. In April, 1908, it especially expressed to him "an appreciation" of his services. On June 11, 1908, the new Master was elected a Trustee, the first and only headmaster (with the exception of Henry Durant, under the special circumstances already described) to hold office since the resignation of Master Moody in 1790.

The years 1907 through 1913 represented for Dr. Ingham and his staff a perilous passage, threatened on the one side by a slim enrollment of boarding students (never until 1913 even approximating the number living at the school at the end of Mr. Ryther's term) and on the other by the obvious fact that more could not be expected until the school's circumstances could be made more secure. In October, 1908, the Master made the following dark report to the Trustees:

> The whole school to date : —
> Day students — 13
> Boarders   — 9

> In money this represents about $4,800 of the $18,000 we need to run the school this year.

In February of 1909, however, Dr. Ingham was able to send the following comment to Edward P. Noyes of the Trustees:

> . . . We find at Dummer a thoroughly equipped plant which will serve without extra expenditures, save for general repairs, for the comfortable housing and instruction of fifty or sixty boys.

> At this time we have about half of the desired number of boarding pupils but the number is increasing steadily and we shall without doubt open next fall with nearly, if not quite our full capacity. We have a large number of excellent teachers, men of special training, force and common sense whose work is winning golden opinions from our patrons.

At this time the faculty consisted of, in addition to Dr. Ingham, five fulltime teachers (including Maurice Lacroix, who taught at Dummer for a total of twenty-one years under four Masters, John Perkins, George Rogers, Perley Horne, and Dr. Ingham — fifteen years under the latter).

The "thoroughly equipped plant," on which more than $50,000 in special gifts had been spent during the preceding ten years, included, in addition to the 330 acres that made up the original farm, the Mansion House, with accommodations for the Headmaster's family and some boys; the Commons, where the kitchen, dining room, and school assembly hall were to be found, as well as rooms for fourteen boys and two masters; Peirce Cottage, a dormitory for twenty-one younger boys and a married master, with facilities for manual training in the basement; the Farm House (now Moody House), renovated and available as a dormitory for five boys and a master; Parsons Schoolhouse, redecorated and re-equipped in 1906; the gymnasium (now converted and forming the frame section of Perkins Dormitory); the Little Red Schoolhouse, in use as a chapel; and a small powerhouse, placed near where the Phillips Building now stands. Electric lights, powered by a succession of school-owned generators, had been in operation with indifferent success since early in 1907.

In spite of the favorable academic and physical climate at the school, however, the economic situation was precarious. A small endowment fund, mostly allocated for special purposes, provided income of slightly more than $1,600 a year. The rest of the cost of running the school had to be raised through tuition charges; when these fell short, all that remained was to seek gifts from friends. In 1908-09 seventeen boarders and six day boys provided an income of $7,863.33, about half what it cost to run the Academy.

In November, 1910, Judge Frederick P. Cabot, Treasurer of the Board and a man to whom Dr. Ingham years later paid handsome tribute, announced that the affairs of the school had reached the point of no return: either the Board must raise $10,000 by April to put matters on a sound footing, or "the affairs of the Academy should be liquidated at the close of the financial year"! The issue was clear-cut. With much to look forward to — and 147 years of service to look back upon — Dummer Academy might have to close its doors.

A major crisis, and a major turning point in the history of the Academy, was reached when on February 16, 1911, Dr. Ingham addressed to Vice-President of the Board Alden P. White (in the absence of President Ambrose) his letter of resignation as a Trustee, expressing his determination not to return another year as Master. This action, and the explanation which Dr. Ingham gave for it, brought to light an issue which had underlain the whole structure and functioning of the Academy since the resignation of Master Moody 121 years earlier and which had for much of that time proven an albatross around the necks of the masters in charge of the school. Nehemiah Cleaveland had put his finger upon the sore place at the close of his remarks in the Appendix to his *Centennial Discourse*. At that time, when the fortunes of the school were at low ebb, he said:

> Even now a man with something of Master Moody's courage and strength, might safely assume the charge, *provided he could have it on similar terms.*

Here lay the core of the problem. Master Moody had, indeed, been complete master of his school and controlled all its workings, established all its policies. With the exception of Nehemiah Cleaveland for a few years during his tenure, no headmaster since had been in this position. With the retirement of Moody, the Trustees, doubtless from the best of motives, took all but the day to day supervision of the school under their own close surveillance and control. At times, as with the unfortunate experiment in 1836-37, from which the school suffered for decades afterwards, their actions bordered on rashness, and were in opposition with the judgment of the man best qualified to express an opinion, the Preceptor. At times, as in 1910-11, perhaps because of the fact that the Trustees were busy men, they tended to default their responsibilities.

Dr. Ingham recognized that if progress were to be made the Board must fulfill its responsibilities, but in cooperation with and under the guidance of a qualified professional teacher at the head of the school. In his letter of resignation he said:

> . . . My reason for wishing to withdraw is simply this, — I cannot get the Trustees, or a working majority of them, to face the problems of the school in a rational, business-like way and I refuse to be party to proceedings where the best efforts of a few are rendered ineffective by the indifference of the majority.
>
> If the Trustees will promptly select a man whom they can and will support, the school will immediately respond to their efforts; it is in every way, the best school we have had, it is growing even at this season and is making friends all about. I sincerely hope the Trustees will co-operate with me, now, at least to the extent required to hold for my successor, the ground so painfully gained during the last three years.

Dr. Ingham's stand was an important one for the Academy's future. There had been Trustees, all along, willing to acknowledge the truth in such a stand.

An appeal letter had already been carefully drawn up by the Board; it now received its more active support. In it the Trustees expressed pride in what the school had been, pride in what it then was and might in the future become; but they evinced a strong disinclination to struggle further under the straitened conditions which had already beset it for some years. Especially did they express their confidence in Dr. Ingham; no more was said about a resignation. In the spring of the year, announcement was made that the campaign had succeeded — narrowly but effectively.

Somewhat over fifty benefactors had brought the school over a dangerous hurdle. The picture had not changed entirely, but it had brightened considerably.

In this same spring wide attention was drawn to the school by an article printed in the April 24 edition of the *Christian Science Monitor*. After presenting a concise historical review, the writer emphasized the fact that it was not merely her noble heritage for which Dummer should be singled out:

> At all events, institutions like the Dummer Academy have one important function, all the more so in a land that is all too prone to hurry, they are monuments. Monuments not of some bygone founder, not of "boys" that did life's work but do it no longer, but monuments to an idea, perhaps we had better say guideposts to it; this idea is that enlightenment is a thing that must be had by brethren for their own and other brethrens' good. This idea can never grow old, nor can it moulder; there is nothing old-fashioned about light.

Particular stress is laid upon the fact that at Dummer the emphasis upon traditional grammar school discipline proffered something of special value to the youth of the day, a day of novelty and innovation in education:

> This, by implication, puts the whole case in a nutshell; no thoroughness is ever lost and nothing thoroughly learned can, by its training, fail to help one, no matter what one's vocation is to be. If a boy learns his grammar thoroughly, it has accustomed him to an exactness of thought that will remain with him whatever his after-work may be and that he will carry into that work when he has to do it.

This argument, familiar (if not always credited) even today when diversification in education grows ever wider, prompted the writer in the *Monitor* to suggest that ". . . other things being equal, it is a question whether a school of this sort, with its more modest scale of expense, and with something that no money can buy or create, a well-defined tradition, be not a better place to send a boy than more elaborate and costly institutions . . ."

In 1911-12 about fifty students, day boys and boarders, were enrolled in the school, well over half of them living on campus. Need was felt for more adequate housing for married faculty, for another dormitory to house fifteen boys and another master, as well, of course, as for increased endowment. Though the financial circumstances were improved, these further gains came slowly. As the result of a welcome offer made to the school in August of 1912 by Miss Ida Mason, a friend of Miss Marion Noyes, the first became a reality. Miss Mason made available $6,000 for the building of a house for a master and his family, to be repaid gradually, with the stipulation that she never be asked to make the loan a gift and with the hope that it would be paid up before other improvements were made. Interestingly enough, the plans for Mason Cottage were drawn up by George Champney, a Dummer graduate in 1902 (who also designed the fourth Byfield Parish Church in 1931).

As the Board looked forward to the 150th anniversary of the founding of the Academy, it chose John Hamilton Morse, a former Trustee and currently President of the Sons of Dummer, to take charge of arrangements. As the year 1912-13 progressed, much attention was focused on these preparations.

With it all, life at the school went on apace. Mrs. Ingham, always a favorite of the boys, was becoming famous for her whist parties. A student council, comprised of a master, two student representatives from Commons and one from Peirce, was formed with the purpose of taking up with the Headmaster "any matters that may be brought up tending to further the happiness or general comfort of the students. . . " The first change brought about by mutual agreement between this group and Dr. Ingham was the moving of the time for evening study from 7:45 up to 7:30, "so that the boys could have a full hour to themselves between study hour and bed time."

Matters outside immediate school life also claimed interest. It appears from *The Archon* that a friend of some of the boys walked all the way down from Exeter, New Hampshire, to pay a visit. David S. Caldwell, member of the Class of '09 and an outstanding runner, having represented the United States in the 1912 Olympic Games, was now at Cornell and continuing his spectacular performances on the track.

The 1913 Dummer basketball team had a highly successful season during which it won every game played on the home floor. An interesting sidelight is the fact that their 25 to 17 win over Melrose High School avenged an earlier loss at Melrose — where the basketball court was diamond-shaped! In the fall there had been too few experienced players to man a football team, so baseball practice had been held instead, including two practice games with Amesbury. The results the following spring were little short of spectacular. In April Chauncey "Doc" Worcester struck out thirteen opposing batters in a row before the Dummer coach mercifully removed him from the game. The team went on to accumulate an impressive series of wins. The success of the season prompted research into the history of baseball at the Academy and unearthed the fact that "rounders" or "catchball" had been played as early as sixty years before (which would have been in the days of Chute and Henshaw).

The year 1913 had been a good one. Little by little under the firm guidance of Dr. Ingham, with the Board of Trustees buckling down to help, the Academy was gaining in strength and appeal. The enrollment approached sixty, with boarders significantly outnumbering the day students. An enthusiasm was growing in the student body, as demonstrated in the following excerpts from *Archon* editorials. (One of the *Archon* editors was Roger B. Coulter, now, since 1949, an active member of the Board of Trustees.)

> This year at Dummer has been very profitable. The number of students is constantly increasing year by year, and with the increase come the good athletes . . . The average standing of the pupils in their marks has been very good . . . There has been no serious case of discipline and the best of feeling has been maintained between the students and the faculty.

> When the lights go out at midnight on the ninth of June, Dummer Academy will have completed one hundred and fifty years of its existence. There is no boarding school for boys in all America (and very few day schools) that have attained to such an age, and no schools of any kind have a more honorable record. . . Dummer does not aim to be a large school, because it has always made a specialty of close attention to the needs of the individual student, but it has always maintained a standard of scholarship equal to the highest. It can easily care for a hundred pupils, and it is steadily growing towards that number.

To celebrate the 150th anniversary of the first opening of the Little Red Schoolhouse by that stern, but warm-hearted old Master

Moody, exactly a century and a half later on March 1, 1913, at the City Club in Boston about seventy-five alumni and friends of the school gathered:

> One of the speakers expressed the belief of all that 'Never since Master Moody combined in his person such powers and effectiveness in many branches has the instruction and discipline been as good, as wide and effective as today. The masters are masters of their subjects and incidentally of the boys.'

> The dominant note emphasized again and again was that 'Dummer should continue a classical preparatory school, doing its work better than any school doing the same sort of work.'

The speakers may be pardoned if in their enthusiasm they overlooked certain estimable contributions that had been made by others since the regime of Master Moody. This was but a preliminary reunion to the grand gathering held at the Academy during Commencement time that June.

Unlike the 100th anniversary in 1863, when the sun shone warmly throughout the day, Commencement Day, June 9, 1913, dawned overcast and threatening and drops of rain fell intermittently during the proceedings. At 10:30 o'clock the Society of the Sons of Dummer held a meeting, electing John Hamilton Morse, Chairman of the 150th anniversary committee, as their President. Dr. Ingham welcomed the throng (over 300 signed the guest book for the occasion) from the platform erected on the lawn between the Mansion House and Commons, calling forward those students who were to receive awards.

On this occasion the presentation of the Morse Flag, the flag which has flown from the flagstaff of the Academy throughout the school year, "to that member of the graduating class whose record in all respects meets with the highest approval of the faculty" was made for the first time. This most coveted award of the school year (donated by the Reverend Glenn Tilley Morse, soon to be elected a Trustee, in memory of an ancestor, Anthony Morse) was given to Roger Brooke Coulter of Sandy Spring, Maryland.

James Hardy Ropes, Hollis Professor of Divinity at Harvard and former President of the Dummer Trustees, spoke briefly. He had served on the Board during the difficult first decade of the century and expressed joy "to see today this place with its strong structure and growth, and may I add, fresh white paint."

Dr. Ingham followed and in the course of his address made very clear the aspirations which he held for the school, those principles which guided his administration throughout twenty-three years at Dummer. His words should be allowed to speak for themselves:

> . . . Governor Dummer founded here a philanthropic institution in many senses, this in particular, that it cannot be a money-making institution, from its very nature. It must give to the student more than it receives from him, at least such has always been the case and I trust always will. When the full history of Dummer is written I venture to prophesy that the world will marvel at the amount of help given to deserving students without apparent resources or means for such work. What has been done in this line, is due to a little band of friends, never numerous, but devoted, who have stood by and helped. . .

> This institution is not only philanthropic, but it is conservative. This is not an educational experiment station, a factory for the grinding out of graduates, but a school where we believe that the mastery of the elements and the development of the power of thinking are of paramount importance. From its beginning the school has been a preparatory classical school, and such in large measure will it continue to be. It also prepares boys for a business career. We believe that the best preparation for college or for business must rest upon the same foundation, namely: ability to express one's self accurately, both orally and in writing, quickness and accuracy in the fundamental operations of mathematics. With that goes the training of the mind, which enables the boy to face the problem of the moment and the training in judgment that tells him when he has solved it. . .

> A community has a right to insist that a school shall serve it in proportion to the outlay involved and the individual student of clean life and honest purpose has a right to expect that he will receive the same attention that the brilliant student, and much more than the brilliant athlete, receives. The school should say to everyone who enters her doors, 'You amount to some-

thing. You can amount to much more than you are. It is your business in life in which we purpose to give you every assistance, to find out that particular work in this world which you can do better than you can do anything else, and to help you to prepare yourself fully to do it . . .'

The orator of the day was the Honorable John D. Long, ex-Governor of Massachusetts and former Secretary of the Navy under President McKinley. Establishing a mood of gentle nostalgia, he dwelt upon the history and heritage of the Academy. Then, looking to the future, he said:

> We must hold every agency to its use. We need the High School and the Academy both, not in competition but in complement of each other. Each is of high value and if wisely adjusted, meets a demand which the other cannot entirely fill.

Following the exercises the company moved to a large tent which had been erected on the tennis courts back of the gymnasium, there to enjoy the commencement dinner. In the course of the festivities, those who had been present at the 100th anniversary, fifty years before, were requested to rise. Seven men and one woman responded. There were a number of after-dinner speakers whose remarks may be read in the published account of the proceedings. One of them, long an interested friend of Dummer Academy as well as eminent Headmaster of a larger and more prominent neighboring school, was Harlan P. Amen of Phillips Exeter Academy. A remark of his points up well the goal for which Dummer Academy, now resurgent, might aim:

> . . . there is a field still for the endowed academies, and I think, a richer and greater field than they have had to work for a century, and it is soon to be available.

Just before the celebration came to an end, the toastmaster, Alden P. White, Vice-President of the Board, called once more upon ex-Governor Long. The Governor ended his brief remarks with a familiar story credited to old Isaac Smith when he was Master of the Academy. The father of one of the boys came to Mr. Smith and inquired when his son would be prepared to enter college. "Well," was the answer, "he will be fitted about the time that you can put a peck of oats into a bushel basket and fill it." — An apt reminder that the chief concern of Dummer Academy was still, as it had always been, the training of boys, and to do that job, it was better fitted in 1913 than it had been for some considerable time.

CHAPTER XI

Charles S. Ingham

In October, 1908, nine boarding students had been reported by Dr. Ingham to the Board. The total enrollment was twenty-two. By December, 1915, the enrollment, having risen to sixty-five, had nearly tripled. The October, 1917, issue of *The Archon* reported the boarding department full, with fifty boys living on campus. Hidden amidst the flamboyant phrasing of a subcommittee report to the Trustees in November, 1919 (the Board was at the time girding itself for a fund-raising drive of startling proportions), is the gratifying statement that the school ". . . is not only full but has a waiting list for the first time probably in the 156 years of its existence [sic]."

In 1908 the total amount spent for faculty salaries, including the Headmaster's, fell short of $5,000. For the year 1915-16, with the teaching staff increased from six to nine, it nearly reached $10,000. In the year 1925-1926, for a faculty of about the same size, Dr. Ingham was authorized to spend $24,000. He himself was earning more than the total amount of the payroll for 1908.

Late in 1910, as we have seen, the Academy tottered on the brink of dissolution. Only a last-ditch fund drive, which barely met the crisis, prevented the closing of the school. The Treasurer's Report for 1914-1915 reflects the comforting fact that the operation of the school broke about even for the year. In September, 1917, Treasurer Frederick P. Cabot was warmly thanked by the Trustees for his report, which was slightly "in the black" for the preceding year. The financial condition of the Academy continued to grow more secure until by June, 1926, the annual operations were showing a healthy margin of safety.

In February, 1922, Charles Somerby, member of the Class of 1913, thereafter a most loyal supporter of Dr. Ingham and the school, and at the time a reporter for the *Haverhill Evening Gazette*, received a letter from Trustee Roland H. Sherman (formerly a student under Master Perkins). In it Mr. Sherman foresaw a happy future for the Academy and described several hoped-for improvements in the plant and the program. Reporting that "for the last few years we have been obliged to turn away from twenty to thirty boys each year for lack of accommodations," he cited the

107

Board's recent vote that facilities at the school be enlarged to provide for a maximum of 100 boys, as compared to the seventy-five or eighty which it could then maintain.

Early in 1926 *The Archon* reported that four new buildings had been built over the past ten years, in addition to a new and better water supply, two tennis courts, and a new athletic field then in process. A strong and influential Student Council had developed; since 1924 *The Milestone* yearbook had become a fixture; *The Archon* itself was flourishing to the tune of twelve issues annually; and the latest popular venture was a dramatics club.

Throughout Dr. Ingham's more than two decades as Headmaster, the Academy showed such steady growth in strength that upon several occasions the Trustees were emboldened to seek funds for capital improvements and for endowment of the school. A puzzling fact is that their efforts were met with very little success. As an immediate outcome of the successful 150th anniversary celebration plans were formed to build a much-needed new dormitory. The architect's drawing showed it to be a solid brick colonial structure; the blueprints called for three classrooms on the ground floor and accommodations for two masters and twenty boys in the upper two stories. It was never built.

To the accompaniment of an emotional exordium in November, 1919, a committee of the Trust unveiled a far more ambitious aspiration — to raise $425,000 for plant improvements and endowment:

> There never was a period in its history when this School needed and was more deserving of financial aid than now. . .With the prevailing unrest that this country is facing; with the lack of real Americanism among a large class of our population; with hundreds of thousands of Aliens trying to break down what we are striving to build up; with the growing tendency to radical socialism, this school plants its feet more firmly than ever on the solid rock of true Democracy; and should do its utmost for the Education of our young men in those patriotic and democratic ideals for which it has always stood. If those schools that have been examples for many years of good citizenship fail us at a crucial time like this, where shall we look for the means to combat the dangers that menace us? The training of a single boy in an institution like this may some day save the

nation from disaster by furnishing the "Man of the Hour"
to meet a great emergency.

By May the Board had decided to eliminate the drive for endowment funds and to reduce the total goal to $200,000 for improve-
ments, to include new classrooms, remodeling for increased dormitory space, and an enlarged athletic plant. Although it does not
appear that the full amount was ever raised as the result of any
single campaign, many of the projects were accomplished over the
next ten years. As late as Commencement-time, 1925, gifts were
still being accepted toward the erection of a $90,000 classroom
building. It, too, was not built; instead, other less ambitious improvements were made.

Perhaps a chief obstacle to the various building plans was fire,
which, though never bringing injury to the boys, was destructive
to property over a period of years. At least one episode of a
lighter nature, however, grew out of one minor conflagration. Late
in 1913 a force of masters and students succeeded in dousing a
fire in Commons, limiting the damage to about $1,000. In the
midst of the confusion the janitor was found steadfastly lighting
the kitchen range. "When asked why he was starting a fire instead
of helping to put one out, he replied that he felt we had enough
help at that, but that they [the students] would soon be hungry,
and if he didn't build the kitchen fire there would be no breakfast.
Breakfast was served on time."

Returning to school at the end of the 1913 Christmas holiday,
the students found a famous old landmark entirely destroyed by
fire. Isaac Smith's old farmhouse, recently remodeled into classrooms and dormitory space, and just refurbished, had burned to the
ground on December 31. Indeed, it was only by dint of strenuous
efforts during this emergency that the Newburyport and Ipswich
fire departments were able to save an even more venerable landmark, the original Little Red Schoolhouse, which stood nearby.
The farmhouse had to be replaced immediately. (In all likelihood,
this accounts for the failure of the Trustees to build the new
dormitory which had been projected immediately following the
150th.)

The Peirce Cottage fire, which occurred early in the morning of
December 12, 1917, could have been serious. "Fire drill" was
carried out smoothly, however; no one was hurt, and many
personal belongings were rescued:

Everything was taken to the Gym and placed in mammoth piles, to be sorted later by the scantily-clad owners. While this was being done, the flames were gradually leveling the Cottage with the ground, and as we stood after returning from a trip to the Gym we saw the walls cave in and the floors drop, and a few moments later the chimneys toppled and fell. It was indeed, a "great" fire, from the kid's point of view; it furnished the requisite amount of flame, amusement, and excitement, to say nothing of its merits as a comedy. The customary ludicrous acts happened: lamps out the window, pillows carefully carried down the stairs. But, aside from the merits of the fire, we must consider what we have lost and how fortunate we were not to have lost our lives.

School was closed early for Christmas. When the boys returned Miss Emily Morgan of Adelynrood had leased to the school the small house nearest the Academy on the Noyes estate. Indeed, this same building was the second schoolhouse, which had been built in 1795 and had passed out of the hands of the Trustees about 1829.

Despite the setbacks over the years, Dr. Ingham doggedly saw to it that the school maintained a steady rate of expansion and improvement. Following the destruction of old Isaac Smith's house, a new building arose in the same spot, modeled after the original structure. Upon its completion in 1915, it was named in honor of the Academy's first Master, the renowned Samuel Moody.

In the same year the basis was laid for a new kind of investment of Academy assets. Arrangement was made to lease Academy pastureland and swampland across the Newburyport Turnpike as the site for a golf course. By one year later the Ould Newbury Golf Club had come into being. In addition to the land improvement and the nominal financial gain which it represents for the school, it has since its establishment extended the privilege of junior membership to students and a welcome outlet during pleasant spring and autumn afternoons to students and faculty alike.

In 1921 the Board for some reason determined to redesignate "Cleaveland Hall" (the sturdy brick colonial dormitory erected following the 1917 fire) "Peirce Hall" after its immediate predecessor. At the same meeting decision was made to name the new brick gymnasium (under construction since August in the space between Peirce and Commons) the Lang Gymnasium. The move

PEIRCE HALL AND THE LANG GYMNASIUM (1952)

was made as a token of appreciation to Mr. William A. Lang, of Melrose, Massachusetts, who had during the summer made the Academy a generous gift of $22,000 in securities. By February of 1922 the new athletic plant was open to inspection; its dedication was a feature of the Commencement proceedings in the spring.

Provision of new gymnasium facilities permitted re-evaluation of the campus setup. The old gymnasium, in use since 1887, was at first to be redesigned for classrooms, and the upper floor of Parsons Schoolhouse was to see service as a dormitory. These plans were changed, and by Commencement, 1925, the old gymnasium, built, according to Master Perkins, by "honest farmers" who put "some of their ruggedness into the structure," had been moved from its longtime resting place behind the Mansion House, across the road to the corner of Elm Street and Middle Road. There it stayed, acquiring an addition in 1944 to accommodate even more boarding students, until once again moved in 1956 to its present location on Middle Road. There it has since been once again remodeled.

Meanwhile the Parsons Schoolhouse remained the chief classroom building; two additional classrooms were supplied by the purchase in 1922 of a Hodgson portable school building, erected behind the gymnasium, between Commons and Mason Cottage. In the same year two tennis courts were constructed back of Peirce Hall, the gift of Trustee Roland Sherman.

A project for many years close to the heart of John Hamilton Morse was brought to the point of action at a Trustees' meeting in March of 1923. As chairman of the committee assigned to study the undertaking, Mr. Morse reported that detailed plans for a new athletic field had been drawn up. Grading was in process during 1924. Seventy-five feet of the back of the huge farm barn behind Moody House was removed to make way. Bleachers were added; and a new entrance, with an imposing stone gateway, took shape. Nearly the entire cost of the operation, which continued into 1927, was borne by John Hamilton Morse, who characteristically made certain that the payment for each phase of the job was in the hands of the Academy before work was started. Mr. Morse demanded almost a free hand with the project, but carried it through with his familiar dynamism — and greatly to the profit of the school. In his original dealings with the Board he gained such firm concessions as to the use of the property surrounding Morse Field that years later, long after his resignation from the Trust, it was necessary to procure his approval of the plans for a new library and classroom building before proceeding with its construction. His resignation came in December, 1928, in the wake of a disagreement over the Academy's financial policies. A man of principle and strong conviction, he proffered this second resignation in the same combative spirit that he had submitted the first, in 1907; but he never, before or after, failed in his basic loyalty to the school.

Almost Mr. Morse's last act before withdrawing had been to plan for the construction of the Academy's stone garage, adjacent to the entrance to Morse Field. In June of 1929 news of still more building was announced. Charles W. Brown, a student at Dummer under Mr. Stanton in 1870, later President of the Pittsburgh Plate Glass Company, had roomed at the Noyes Boarding House while attending the school. In memory of his good friend Edward Parish Noyes, hardworking Trustee of the Academy from 1895 until his death in 1913, Captain Brown (he had been master of his own merchant ship at the age of twenty) provided funds for the construction of the Edward P. Noyes Memorial Library. Dedicated at the Commencement of 1930, the new brick colonial library has been aptly described as possessing an "unpretentious distinction." So constructed that the basement could be equipped as a workshop for the boys, it provided in the main reading room upstairs a handsome fireplace, natural mahogany bookshelves, and "fine old beams saved when the ancient barn of the Academy farm was demolished."

Among the gifts to the Academy not so far mentioned, at least two deserve attention. One was a contribution by members of the Ingham family in memory of the late Samuel Kellog Ingham of Saybrook, Connecticut. In the form of securities valued at $5,400, the income was to be applied "in such ways as will from year to year cause to be remembered the name of a plain man who feared God. . ." The second had, like its counterpart in 1929, been given in honor of Edward Parish Noyes. Received in December, 1914, not long after the death of Mr. Noyes, it had amounted to $17,140, the gift of Joseph Lee, at the time a member of the Boston School Board. Part of the money made possible the rebuilding of Moody House; the balance established the Edward Parish Noyes Foundation, the income from which was to be applied to the pay of an instructor at the Academy.

As the Academy became settled on a stronger and sounder basis, life in the school continued to focus upon those sturdy principles set forth by Dr. Ingham in the course of the 150th anniversary celebration. Nevertheless, it had its lighter side as well. *The*

Archon for February, 1915, reports, contentedly, the following: "Quite a while ago Mrs. Ingham started having tea served Sunday afternoons. Since then these little functions have become the main support of our Sunday afternoons, and we look forward to them eagerly." On the more active side, the basketball team for 1916 turned in an undefeated season, including a close squeak over Hamilton High School, 13 to 12, and a shut-out of the Newburyport YMCA, 24 to 0! In the same year the Senior Dance was, from all accounts, a smashing success. The gay couples danced to a seven piece orchestra (including two "banjo-mando-lins"!), and the ladies took home as souvenirs of the event "white leather dance orders which were made in the form of coin purses":

> The order of dances consisted of eight one-steps, eight foxtrots, and four waltzes. Although the floor was slightly crowded with the forty-five couples, everyone seemed to have room enough for their varied steps.

World War I had its effect upon the school. Each year, in response to the Headmaster's request that the students "deprive themselves of something in order to aid these suffering people across the sea," the boys provided generously for war relief funds. In 1917 regular military instruction was recognized as a part of the school course. In June of that year, as well as the next, the Dummer Academy Company, consisting of six squads of eight men each, marched in the Memorial Day parade in Newburyport, drawing congratulations from G. A. R. headquarters on their "very military bearing and appearance." Gardens were planted and fruit trees were cultivated on the Academy grounds by the boys. During the summer of 1918 girls from Radcliffe College lived in the Commons and farmed Academy land. A feature of the 1921 Commencement activities was the dedication of a World War I Soldiers' Memorial plaque, placed by the Town of Newbury on a large boulder at the intersection of Elm and Middle Streets. Of the sixty-four names embossed upon it, six were of Dummer boys.

To confirm that schoolboys in 1918 were very much like those in 1818 (and, doubtless, like those-to-be in 2018), it may be well to adduce the following theme, quoted from the January *Archon:*

> One hot, drowsy June morning, I sat in Study Hall. I thought I had prepared my lessons and I had a period to forget them in. I sat counting the cars of a far away freight train, until Mr. La Croix suggested that I might get to work. I took out a pencil and paper, and played noughts and crosses with myself. A fly walked across

my desk, and I immediately swatted him with my pencil.
He was hurt, so I gave him artificial respiration. After
a while he was able to crawl, and then I took him on my
pencil and taught him to fly. At first he fell on the desk
but on the second trial he flew merrily away. I was quite
lonesome after he had left, so I drew a playmate for
myself. He wasn't very good-looking, being lop-sided,
so I erased him. Suddenly a horrible thought struck
me, — I had entirely forgotten about a theme for Mr.
Horne and had fifteen minutes in which to write it!
Life's like that!

The April, 1920, issue of *The Archon* describes a lively winter
outing involving a crisp three-hour sleigh ride to the famous Bald-
pate Inn in Georgetown; then apple cider and a piping hot dinner
to steel the boys for the long ride home; and finally a welcome
retreat to warm beds for the night.

More changes accompanied the passage of time. By 1923 the
familiar trolleys had disappeared, their function partially supplied
by the "wonderful new cement turnpike" which passed by the
school. The school garage boasted seven automobiles. Late in
this year moving picture shows began to replace the home-grown
minstrel shows and professional lectures which had provided the
bulk of the week-end entertainment for many years.

At the end of fifteen years of arduous and unstinting effort at
the Academy, Dr. Ingham was granted by the Board a leave of
absence, at about half pay, for the school year 1922-23. Brought
to Dummer as acting Headmaster for just that year was Mr. Carl
Nestor Holmes, a graduate of Dartmouth College and most recently
an instructor at the Fessenden School in West Newton. The year
passed smoothly. Nevertheless, the editors of the 1923 yearbook,
who dedicated their publication to Dr. Ingham, described a warm
homecoming welcome for the Headmaster at the year's end:

> The cheers which shook the Commons building, on the
> evening of his return, were proof enough of how much
> we have all missed him, and how gladly we greet him
> and Mrs. Ingham back to Dummer once again.

In the early fall of 1925, on a beautiful afternoon in late September, the casual passerby might have imagined that he had somehow stumbled 200 years backward in history. From his vantage
point at the base of a verdant natural amphitheatre (where the
parking area behind the Phillips Building now is), he would have

witnessed the arrival of a handsome coach and four at the top of the knoll, a few yards in front of Peirce Hall. From its interior, in startling realism, undeniably 18th century ladies and gentlemen would have emerged, to be greeted by a most gracious couple who could be no other than Lieutenant Governor William Dummer and his lady.

More startling yet, amongst the little pines studding the bank of the lovely "theatre" fleeting glimpses of Norridgewock savages might have been had, or the chilling sight of Father Sebastian Ralé, the English-hating French priest. In due time, the portly and comfortable figure of Master Samuel Moody would make its appearance, followed by many of his illustrious pupils. Not until the arrival of the spare and bearded figure of Father Time, stalking across the green, accompanied by four dancing maidens, would the viewer have been returned to reality — and the realization that what he was witnessing was, after all, a pageant.

Sponsored by the Dummer Allies, the loyal ladies of Dummer, this remarkable production had wide publicity and such wide success that a repeat performance, somewhat augmented, was presented one year later. The weather smiled benignly on both occasions:

> . . .The day was perfect, a clear blue sky overhead and the air was balmy. Outdoor pictures of living characters, historic scenes of colonial days were excellently presented. The audience was large and received the presentation most enthusiastically. . .

Over fifty people, authentically costumed and carefully directed, appeared in the various scenes devised and written by one of the ladies. Appropriately, the Secretary of the Academy Trust, Joseph N. Dummer, portrayed his ancestor, Richard Dummer. Equally fitting, Dr. and Mrs. Ingham appeared as the Governor and his lady, their long-ago predecessors in the Mansion House. The Reverend Glenn Tilley Morse made an impressive Samuel Moody, while other members of the Board and of the faculty played a variety of roles.

The Pageant, ambitiously conceived and painstakingly executed, told of the story of the coming of the white man to New England; of staunch, warm-hearted Richard Dummer; and of his generous-minded grandson, William. It depicted the founding of the school under the firm and kindly eye of Master Moody. From start to finish it was peopled with personalities long a part of the

Dummer legend. A musical background enlivened the scenes and accompanied the dances which were pleasantly interwoven with the theme. Friends and neighbors, Trustees and faculty, Dummer boys and young ladies of the neighborhood played large parts and small in contributing to the popular success of so fitting a memorial to the ancient traditions in which the school and the community had their roots. The Dummer Pageant, a high point in the years 1925 and 1926, must, indeed, have presented an intriguing and colorful spectacle.

In his valedictory address at the 1930 Commencement exercises, Dr. Ingham spoke not only of the friends and neighbors of the school, with whom he and Mrs. Ingham had developed so many common interests and concerns over the past 23 years, but also of those responsible with him for the progress made at the institution. His gratitude extended to the Trustees and the alumni, among whom he especially cited Frederick H. Goodwin, one of his own boys, who became for twenty-nine years a member of the Board and who remains a loyal friend of the Academy. Particularly, however, he emphasized the members of his faculty, "who do the actual work and are blamed often and seldom praised. . . " As an example of the latter he cited Walter J. Farrell, with him for eighteen years, for most of them as Assistant to the Headmaster. A graduate of Boston University, at the Academy he taught mathematics and Latin, coached a variety of teams, served as Athletic Director and Faculty Advisor to *The Archon*, and at one time or another performed almost every function relating to the responsibilities of the faculty. Assistant to Dr. Ingham before Mr. Farrell had been the Reverend George Frederic Degen, a man of wide experience in school work before coming to Dummer. While at Dummer, from 1911 through 1915, Dr. Degen not only taught classes, but took wide responsibility for the enrollment of new boys. When he left the Academy, it was to become Headmaster of his own school in Portland, Maine.

Born and educated in France, but eventually settled on a small farm near Dummer Academy, Maurice La Croix was entering upon his seventh year as a member of the faculty when Dr. Ingham came to South Byfield. He remained in spite of offers of positions in larger schools, through twenty-one years of teaching at Dummer, until forced to retire, beloved by all, because of ill health. Also among those longest with Dr. Ingham was Francis J. Reagan, from 1916 an assistant in the administration, a coach, and a teacher of commercial subjects.

DR. CHARLES S. INGHAM

It would be difficult to represent fairly here those among the Trustees upon whom the Headmaster could lean most heavily. Some, like Edward Parish Noyes, John Hamilton Morse, and Roland Sherman, have already been mentioned. The one man particularly singled out by Dr. Ingham was Frederick Marden Ambrose, a summertime neighbor of the school. Elected to the Board in 1895, a Dummer graduate in 1875, Mr. Ambrose remained a tireless and generous member until his death shortly after the resignation of Dr. Ingham. Chosen President by the Board at the same meeting during which Dr. Ingham was appointed Master, he retained this function for sixteen years, relinquishing it in 1923, but continuing a Trustee. The strength and support which he represented are best described by the Headmaster together with whom he strove so long to re-establish the school on a sound basis:

> A man of tireless energy, faultless enthusiasm and generosity, his share in the progress of this school is above all praise. In the hard days of 1907 and on, I never turned to him in vain. He saw with prophetic eye the advances that have been made and foretold those that are to come. Dummer cannot repay him, and personally in good days and bad . . . he was a friend such as few men find.

There will be opportunity hereafter to give mention to other members of the Board whom Dr. Ingham must have had in mind in expressing his appreciation for the work of the Trustees: among them Joseph N. Dummer, elected Secretary of the Board in Dr. Ingham's first year and still holding that trust for years after Ingham's departure; the Reverend Glenn Tilley Morse, donor of the Morse Flag Award and restorer of the Little Red Schoolhouse; and James Duncan Phillips, who, joining the Board near the end of Dr. Ingham's tenure, was to be instrumental in the continued upsurge of the school.

The way up had been long and hard, but over a twenty-three year period there had been no cessation in the pursuit of a sound school and a productive educational program. In October, 1929, Dr. Ingham conveyed to the Board his desire to retire at the end of the school year. He and Mrs. Ingham — their children grown and established, their school far better provided and far better supported than when they had first come to it — looked forward to traveling abroad. The vigorous and confident young man of

1907 had over the years acquired a kind of tempered strength which, with his unshaken determination, had seen the Academy through difficult, even threatening, times:

> . . .He took the school in badly demoralized condition
> . . . he has given twenty-three years of serious and vital
> effort to its upbuilding, and has brought it back from
> the verge of dissolution to a successful and progressive
> institution fitted for a long period of usefulness.

Such was the estimate of the Board, written into its record on January 28, 1930. Dr. Ingham had brought the Academy to the verge of its greatest period of service since the days of Master Moody. Announcement of the identity of the man who was to see it through the next twenty-nine remarkable years appeared for the first time in the Trustees' records, a twin to the preceding entry, on January 28, 1930. A young instructor from the faculty of Deerfield Academy, his name was Edward W. Eames.

CHAPTER XII

Edward W. Eames

Early in the school year 1930-31, the first of a succession of constructive and creative changes that was to span Ted Eames's headmastership came into force. With practically the unanimous concurrence of Trustees, alumni, masters and boys, a campaign was begun to provide that ancient Dummer Academy henceforth be generally known as *Governor Dummer Academy*. Far from seeming a reckless abandonment of a time-honored title, the new name appeared a long overdue tribute to the school's founder, the King's Lieutenant Governor William Dummer. For far too long the significance of the name Dummer had been lost upon all but those intimate with the history of the school. Thereafter all who became friends of the Academy were to be urged to refer to it as *Governor Dummer*. The newspapers were requested to employ the new title in their reports. The letter insignia for athletic award winners became a large "G" instead of the familiar "D." Sports writers, quick to seize upon convenient tags, almost immediately began to refer to the teams as "the Governors."

Whether certain tales relating to the change are apocryphal is not an issue. Their point is clear. According to one of them, the student newspaper at Andover, *The Phillipian,* had once published the following headline: "Andover Plays Dummer Team." Shortly afterward, so the story goes, *The Exonian* at Phillips Exeter quoted the headline and followed it with the terse comment: "Impossible." It is rumored, too, that Mr. Eames was mildly chagrined at the reaction of some of his more puckish friends to one newspaper headline announcing his appointment as Headmaster: "Eames Accepts Dummer Post." Certainly there was ample historical justification for the new name, but, in addition, one strongly senses relief in the alacrity with which all who were closely connected with the school adopted it. The name Governor Dummer Academy, greeted with enthusiasm in 1930, became, by Act of the Massachusetts Legislature and acceptance of the Academy's Board of Trustees, the official corporate title in 1950.

In December, 1930, Mr. Eames, as guest editorial writer for the school magazine, *The Archon,* paid tribute to the work of his predecessor, Dr. Ingham, and in so doing highlighted the important contributions of the retired Headmaster during his twenty-three years at the Academy. It was pointed out that under his guidance enrollment in the school had grown from literally nothing when he first took over to an average of between seventy and eighty-five boarding students in the 'twenties. A faculty of nine about doubled what it had been at the start. The campus, still the original 330 acres provided by the Governor almost 200 years earlier, had been judiciously improved with the leasing of a portion for the establishing of a golf course, and the planting of many vines and trees, particularly the pines on the hill beyond where Ingham House now stands. Of these trees Dr. Ingham writes (in an entertaining and informative series of notes which he has left concerning the campus trees):

> The 20,000 little pines on Broadback Hill south of the school, set out 1920-1930, will give the school a wonderful grove if they escape blister rust, top weavil, and especially *cigarette butts*. 'Ware fire!

The warning is well taken.

The growth of the school required more facilities. The second Peirce Hall, Lang Gymnasium, Perkins Dormitory (the old gymnasium moved and remodeled), the Noyes Library and Mason Cottage stand as evidence of Dr. Ingham's efforts in this direction. Before his retirement his achievements were underscored by the fact of his election as Vice-President of the Headmasters Association, a nationwide association limited to 100 members, all prominent headmasters and principals in private and public secondary schools.

"As an educator," wrote Mr. Eames, "Dr. Ingham believed in the old-fashioned classical training reached through good teaching and hard study":

> His standards of scholarship were high and he enjoyed particular success as a trainer of young teachers. His understanding of boys, too, was keen and penetrating, as was revealed in the brief characterizations which he handed to his seniors on Commencement Day along with their diplomas. In short, he was, in the best sense of that old phrase, "a gentleman and a scholar."

> It seems to me peculiarly fitting then, that we should now through the medium of our school paper acknowledge even in part our debt to Dr. Ingham, a fine and

good man, who has just closed his long and devoted service as Headmaster of Governor Dummer Academy.

Dr. Ingham had found the school at low ebb and had brought it through perilous times to see it become a vigorous and respected institution. Such was the legacy accepted by the new headmaster.

Mr. Eames found himself at the head of a school potentially stronger than for many, many decades — yet facing, with the rest of the nation, a devastating economic depression and the threat of financial collapse. He undertook immediately to build solidly on the existing foundation. There was much to be done: faculty to be hired; students to be enrolled (of the sixty-eight in attendance in the spring of 1930, only thirty were to return in the fall); and improvements to be made in the physical condition of the school. In order to carry out the improvements which he felt were necessary to begin the new year in the right way, Mr. Eames got from the Trustees a fund of $20,000. Arriving at the school early in the summer and bringing with him one administrative assistant, he pitched into the task he had envisioned. During the summer months there was activity in every corner of the campus. By fall, $19,576.81 of the $20,000 had been carefully expended.

On the recommendation of Dr. Ingham a new heating system was installed in the Mansion House and additional electrical and plumbing improvements made. The venerable Commons Building came in for extensive repairs in lighting, plumbing, carpentry, and decorating. Individual base plugs were installed in the boys' rooms to provide for desk lamps. In particular, the living room, which had served as a common room for the school, was attractively redecorated to permit its use for vesper services, evening meetings, and other gatherings. "When a fire is blazing merrily in the fireplace, the room is a cheerful one even on the most gloomy days," reported *The Archon* early in the fall. Peirce, Perkins, and Moody, too, came in for their share of attention. Even Morse Field was not overlooked; a new set of bleachers was constructed for use at football and baseball games.

Perhaps the most general improvement, however, was in the refurnishing of the boys' rooms. With some help from one of the first appointees to the faculty, Thomas McClary Mercer (to whom Governor Dummer boys have, since the beginning, ascribed awesome powers!), the new headmaster was able to procure sturdy and handsome new equipment for every room:

> The boys' rooms in the dormitories have . . . been provided with Colonial furniture suggestive of the period of the founding of the school. Every room has been furnished with a maple bedstead, bureau, desk, and chair modeled after early Colonial pieces. Color is provided by the borders on the Monk's cloth window drapes and bed spread.

Space does not allow review here of the painstaking attention given to putting the Academy into efficient condition for opening in the fall of 1930. The arrival of boys and parents in September, however, was marked by enthusiastic expressions of admiration and appreciation.

The nucleus of a faculty was formed early; how well this was accomplished will appear clearly in the passage of years. Two members of the faculty for the previous year were to return: Mr. Francis Reagan, who had been an administrative assistant to Dr. Ingham and who taught commercial subjects; and O. P. "Pep" Nash, a popular and volatile instructor in French. Furthermore, with characteristic foresight and forethought, Mr. Eames had by the beginning of the summer already appointed four others to the teaching staff. Of these, three were to play key roles in the continued resurgence of the Academy: Mr. Mercer, a graduate of Centre College, with an M.A. from Harvard; Mr. William B. Jacob, a graduate of Bowdoin; and Mr. Edgar D. Dunning, B.S., Union College, M. A., Princeton University. Before the end of this first year, two more particularly significant additions were to be made: first, Arthur W. Sager, B.A., Bates College; and a few months later A. Macdonald Murphy, B.A., Harvard. In addition to the new headmaster, eleven men made up the working faculty for 1930-31.

With all of this activity, there were still boys to be enrolled for the opening of school. Most of the boys who had been attending the Academy at the end of the previous school year were not returning. Nevertheless, in Mr. Eames's first year, there were ninety students, sixty of them boarders, thirty-two from outside of Massachusetts. Boarding facilities were taxed to the utmost. Boys were living on the top floor of the Mansion House once again, while seven boys and a master lived in the old Noyes Boarding House on Elm Street, by then the private residence of Miss Helen McGregor Noyes, a good friend of the school.

Experience and judgment led the new headmaster to incorporate a number of changes in the program during that first year, some of which demand mention. With the thought that the student body would be happier and more productive if it could occupy itself with worth-while activities beyond the expected studying and athletics, he added certain outlets to those which had already existed, like *The Archon* and the Sunday afternoon teas in the Mansion House. Under the leadership of Mr. Jacob, the Outing Club was formed and made trips to such points of interest as the Mount Washington area and Chocorua, where the boys were able to explore on skiis, snow shoes, or on foot. Under the gifted guidance of Mr. Sager, the activity of the orchestra was expanded, and the Governor Dummer Glee Club started a tradition of excellence that has become a byword with all who have come to know the Academy. Saturday evening entertainment was established on a weekly basis and ranged from excellent programs by entertainers or lecturers to silent movies.

The Evening Meeting was instituted as an important part of school day. In those early days in the living room of Commons, the boys sat on the floor, facing the fireplace (as they still do today in the Cobb Room of the Phillips Building). Primarily for the purpose of making important school announcements, Evening Meetings have come to have many other functions as well. Occasionally a visitor, perhaps an alumnus, or dean of admissions from one of the colleges, is asked to say a few words. More frequently faculty-member coaches or team captains report on the heroics of their squads. Or who can forget the pandemonium that lets loose when the Headmaster, on rare and spectacular occasions, announces a "Free Day"!

Sunday Evening Vespers Prove Pleasant Addition to School Life

An addition made this fall to the weekly program of the school is the regular Sunday evening Vespers Service. At a few minutes before eight o'clock, the entire student body together with the faculty gather in the living room of the Commons where chairs are carefully arranged to accommodate all. Neighbors and friends of the school, as well as parents of the boys, are guests. At the head of the room, the brightly burning fireplace fire and the soft candle light help to create a homelike atmosphere.

The service itself closely resembles the old New England family song service which was held around the fireplace. It consists mainly of the singing of familiar hymns. There is a responsive reading followed by a short, informal, inspirational talk either by a minister or by some other friend of the school. The service closes each week with the same two hymns: "Dear Lord and Father of Mankind" and "Now the Day is Over."

So begins a report in the first *Archon* of 1930-31. To one who has lived and worked at Governor Dummer, as to innumerable alumni, parents and friends, these Sunday evening ceremonies stand out as an especially pleasant and welcome way to end the weekend and begin the new week.

In this same year it became the custom to follow varsity athletic encounters against visiting teams with a formal reception for players, parents, and friends of either school. At these functions students, faculty members and guests can mingle pleasantly, discussing the afternoon's errors and achievements, and making or renewing acquaintances. In athletic contests, the Academy was continuing the trend started by Dr. Ingham in later years, attempting to schedule neighboring schools of comparable size and purpose: Roxbury Latin, Deerfield, Lawrence Academy, Brooks School, Tabor Academy, Belmont Hill, Milton Academy, Browne and Nichols, Thayer Academy, and Moses Brown appear on the schedules that first year, in addition to larger institutions like Phillips Academy and the Harvard Freshmen.

The man who with remarkable sureness of touch was guiding this enrichment of the school program had first been brought to the notice of the full Board by their hard-working colleague James Duncan Phillips, chairman of the committee appointed by President Alden P. White to find a successor to Dr. Ingham. Tenacious when pursuing a goal which he deemed worth-while, Mr. Phillips had heard, through friends, of a young Amherst graduate on the staff of Deerfield Academy who was ambitious to have a school of his own; but he had not been successful in determining the young man's name. A telephone call to Dr. Frank L. Boyden, redoubtable Headmaster at Deerfield and even at that time a dean among the private school headmasters of the nation, elicited an invitation to visit — but still no name. Dr. Boyden was clearly prepared to ward off any unworthy offers that might be made to one of his protégés.

It took very little time for Mr. Phillips to convince the Deerfield

Louis Huntress

GOVERNOR DUMMER ACADEMY'S YOUTHFUL HEADMASTER:
EDWARD W. EAMES

headmaster that the opening at Byfield was a good one. In fact, the two men parted in mutual respect, and it was not long before Dr. Boyden was proffered, and had accepted, an invitation to join the Board of Trustees of the Academy. The acquisition, as a Trustee, of a man of so much wisdom and experience in the successful administering of a private academy was, in itself, an important achievement for the school.

The interview between James Duncan Phillips and the young Deerfield master Edward W. Eames must, unquestionably, have had all the elements of a highly skilled debate, for both were men of firm principles and each was determined to be associated with a school which would represent the best to be had in private secondary education.

During that autumn in 1929 Ted Eames, with his wife Eleanor, had been making occasional drives through the Berkshire hills, looking for a spot where he might, without a great deal of capital, establish a small private school. After six and a half years of exacting training at Deerfield and with clear convictions derived therefrom, he was eager to strike out on his own.

Just as Mr. Phillips had convinced Dr. Boyden, he was able to satisfy this young master's searching questions — and to satisfy himself, as well, that here was the man for the job. From this point it was not difficult to bring the matter before his committee and then the full Board of Dummer Academy. On January 28, 1930, Edward W. Eames was unanimously elected Headmaster, to assume charge of the school on July 1.

Ted Eames was born on August 14, 1900, in Buffalo, New York, son of businessman Edward A. Eames and Isabel Morey Eames, who until her death in 1958, at the age of eighty-three, remained a particularly staunch and active supporter of her son and of his school. Graduating from the Nichols Country Day School in Buffalo, he entered Amherst in 1918, where he amassed a most distinguished record. A leader in his class, member of the Beta Theta Pi fraternity, he was inducted into Phi Beta Kappa in his junior year. By his election to the Presidency of the Student Council and his appointment as Class Marshal, he accomplished two of the highest honors of the college. He played on the soccer, basketball, and baseball teams — and ended his college career by graduating with high honors. This combination of athletic, academic, and leadership qualities form the hard core of the personality which ignited the surge which has brought Governor Dummer

Academy to the forefront in private secondary school education over the past three decades.

A brief attendance at the Harvard Law School was sufficient to decide Mr. Eames against a legal career. In the spring of 1923 his on-the-job-training — training of the highest order — was begun at Deerfield Academy. After a little more than three years, the young instructor took a year off to qualify for a Master's Degree in English at Harvard. At the Widener Library, where she was employed, he met Eleanor Kimball, of Burlington, Vermont; and in 1926 they were married. The wife of a boarding school headmaster has, besides her obligations in the home, an active responsibility in her husband's work. From the outset Eleanor Eames has been an inexhaustible source of encouragement and help in her husband's career.

Alert, thoughtful, tried and proven in the fires of one of New England's leading academies, Ted Eames, although only thirty years old, was admirably qualified to assume leadership in a school of his own.

Thus, early in the summer of 1930, moving with that long, striding gait from one scene of activity to another across a campus echoing with sounds of preparations for the fall opening of school, the lean, erect figure of the young headmaster could be descried. Vigorous and energetic, he combined with these qualities the counter-balancing deliberateness and single-minded concentration on the matter at hand that have been so characteristic of him throughout the years. On each problem he appeared to focus the full force of practical logic, and in his deliberate, almost drawling manner of speaking to encompass unerringly each smallest detail. Strength and precision, tempered by a genuine concern for individual human beings, these qualities have, perhaps more than any other, characterized the dogged and brilliant leadership which enabled Edward W. Eames to bring Governor Dummer Academy so far — with so much credit to himself and to those who have worked closely with him.

On June 7, 1931, Governor Dummer Academy graduated twenty-three seniors, of whom seventeen planned to go on to college. In the Commencement program that spring some significant differences from previous years were effected. Baccalaureate at the Adelynrood Chapel on the preceding Sunday, the Ambrose Prize Speaking Contest, and the Morse Flag presentation were held as usual. But on the evening preceding the graduation ceremonies a Senior Sing was held, with the entire school, together with parents and friends, gathered on Sunset Hill overlooking the northwest corner of the main campus. "This simple but unusual ceremony ranks as one of the most impressive parts of the Commencement exercises," reported *The Archon:*

> . . .The large group formed a circle around an open fire, and as the sun sank slowly below the horizon amid brilliant colors, many well-known college, school, and folk songs were sung.

After the announcement of the class gift and the dedication of the *Milestone,* the Sing came to a close:

> The seniors in caps and gowns, then descended the hill while the undergraduates sang the *Senior Song.* Reaching the Milestone, they filed slowly around the historic marker and responded to the watchers at the top of the hill with the same strains. . .

Today this rendering of the *Senior Song,* with first the underclassmen taking up the chorus from their seats on the lawn in front of the Mansion House, and then the members of the graduating class as they file around the Milestone, has become the climactic event in the graduation itself.

The musical clubs performed a concert in Lang Gymnasium at noon. Following luncheon served on the lawn in front of the Mansion House and in Commons came the baseball game. At six o'clock in the evening the activities of the day culminated in the first annual Commencement Dinner. Although held initially in Lang Gymnasium, as the throng of interested alumni, friends, and neighbors of the Academy has grown through the years the dinner has been moved into a huge tent pitched on Morse Field, and most recently into the capacious new Memorial Gymnasium. Here, after a delightful meal enlivened with comments by a genial toastmaster and climaxed by group singing led by Mr. Sager, there are customarily a pair of challenging and highly entertaining speakers. The growth in popularity, among friends of the school, of this annual event symbolizes, perhaps as much as any other one thing, the respect in which the Governor Dummer Academy program in general has come to be held.

The story of the next several years at the Academy is, first and foremost, the story of an amazing and dynamic growth in which everyone connected with the school seemed to have a part. A key factor in this growth is the spontaneous enthusiasm of the boys themselves, who supported every project and, indeed, on some occasions, assumed a leadership role. The Class of 1932 supplied the labor to dig nine hundred feet of ditches to prepare proper drainage for portions of Morse Field, every senior spending several hours in the trenches during May. The following fall, after twenty boys directed by Mr. Dunning and Mr. Kirk of the faculty had done the preliminary work, sixty boys voluntarily devoted their athletic period every afternoon between the Thanksgiving recess and the Christmas holidays to constructing an earthen dam eighty feet long and five feet high to provide the school with a second hockey rink in the low land in front of where Ingham House now stands.

The trend continued. Again in the fall of 1933 a small group of boys made necessary preparations for a new board running track, sixteen laps to the mile. Although some boys spent more time than others, every student in school had a significant part in bringing this ambitious project to completion.

In December, 1934, six boys began to meet in the evenings in Moody House with Philip H. Cobb, a member of the faculty and a remarkable boys' man. As a natural consequence of the work projects already completed, it was the proposal of these boys that the students in the school organize a campaign to raise money for a new building to relieve the crowding of facilities in the dining room, living room, and kitchen of Commons.

On January 17, 1935, the "Secret Six," as they have come to be known, met with the Headmaster to explain their plan. Enthusiastically Mr. Eames entered into the project and, after careful consideration of the practical problems, suggested a few modifications. The student committee was enlarged to get a wider sampling of opinion. Shortly afterward, on the evening of a "Free Day," the "Secret Six" carefully outlined their hopes before the entire student body. The Trustees, informed of the events, pledged their aid and support, and expressed to the students their appreciation of the boys' loyalty to the school.

The country was still in the depths of the Depression. It was decided to go slowly and to promote the campaign without professional assistance. A Committee on the Student Campaign was formed, comprising the original six boys and eight additional members. Each of the "Secret Six" was named chairman of one of the working committees: Committee on Alumni, Committee on Building, Committee on Time Schedule, Committee on Location, Committee on Records, and Committee on Publicity. The first act of the last-named group was to issue a carefully planned issue of *The Archon,* attractively describing the school and the new plans for expansion, "in order to assist the boys of the school in the part which they are playing in raising funds for a new building."

As the student-initiated campaign gathered momentum during the next few months, other changes were coming over the campus. Looking to a record enrollment of 119 boys in the fall of 1934, including ninety-six boarders, the need for increased boarding facilities, as well as housing for a married master, was pressing. Recently elected President of the Board, James Duncan Phillips made available money to erect a building behind Commons and opposite Mason Cottage to be named Duncan House after his grandfather. This new residence provided space for a married faculty member and his family, and, on the second floor, accommodations for nine boys. In addition, two much-needed classrooms were constructed in the basement.

Meanwhile, the sum of $200,000 had been established as the goal for the New Building campaign, the largest portion of the amount to be set aside to build, furnish, and partially endow the new structure, with $25,000 to be devoted to remodeling the kitchen and dining areas in Commons for use as a Master's apartment and rooms for thirteen boys. Early in the fall of 1934 an Advisory Committee for the campaign was formed, comprised of twelve distinguished men and the members of the Board of Trustees. It included such members as the chairman, Dr. Lewis Perry, Headmaster of Phillips Exeter Academy; and the Honorable John G. Winant, former Governor of New Hampshire. Mr. Dunning of the Academy faculty was appointed Executive Secretary for the campaign. Under the auspices of this committee, and with generous support from other friends of the school, a handsome campaign bulletin was printed in February, 1935. Containing an introductory statement signed by three of New England's outstanding educators, Dr. Perry, Dr. Boyden of Deerfield, and Dr. Claude Moore Fuess, Headmaster of Phillips Academy at Andover (the last two, members of Governor Dummer's Board of Trustees), this informative and beautifully illustrated booklet provided visual support for the official kick-off of the drive, which came on February 28.

Because of the immediate need for adequate kitchen and dining room facilities, the Board decided in September, 1935, to start the wing of the New Building as soon as sufficient funds were available. The following June the work began. On September 30, the opening day of school for the new year, dinner was served for the first time in the new dining hall. Designed by Walter H. Kilham of Boston, a man who in serving the Academy in succeeding years took a real interest in the school and earned, in return, the respect and affection of masters and boys, the magnificently equipped new wing was an attractive, as well as a highly serviceable, unit. It provided, among other things, a large fireplace at one end of the dining hall, in front of which the Vesper services and other school meetings could be held until the completion of the remainder of the building.

During the same summer an important purchase and gift resulted in a significant addition to the acreage belonging to the Academy. Thirty-six acres, two frame dwellings, a garage and three barns were acquired partly by purchase from the trustees of the old Noyes Farm, and partly by the substantial gift of one of those trustees, George N. Whipple, who had graduated from the Academy in 1874. In time for the opening of school in 1937 the farm cottage was completely remodeled to accommodate another married master and his family and to serve as a dormitory for six boys. Since then the second dwelling house has been converted to house members of the school's kitchen and house-keeping staff. The other buildings have been indispensable to the maintenance department for storage and shop area, as well as providing space for a machine shop program for the boys. Much of the land has since been developed into four tennis courts and the extensive Whipple Athletic Fields.

In every sense the Academy was growing. The July 1, 1938, issue of *The Archon,* in reviewing the school year just past, reported another record enrollment, 139 boys, including 123 boarding students, among whom were boys from Northern Ireland, Guatemala, and Germany. It is interesting to note that with Mr. Eames's arrival at Governor Dummer the mid-summer issue of this school magazine, containing reprints of the most interesting articles and pictures from the year's editions, replaced the school catalogue. Each year this copy of *The Archon* provided those interested in the Academy with a unique insight into the real life and purposes of the school.

The keystone of the educational structure which Mr. Eames was developing at Governor Dummer was, and has always remained, a sound and productive academic program. The strength of this

THE WHIPPLE ATHLETIC FIELD
Northwest corner of the campus

program has from the very beginning derived in large part from the excellence of the teaching faculty, but it found its direction and much of its value in the convictions of the Headmaster. These convictions he stated through the years as often and by as many means as possible. In the course of a speech delivered off campus in 1947, Mr. Eames (by then, Dr. Eames) made the following comments:

> . . . Five-sixths of our American teen-age boys and girls attend some sort of secondary school. Of these boys and girls, more than half simply are not working to capacity.
>
> Now, if this is true, and I think it is, we ought to be concerned. Every good teacher knows that what counts most is not learning, but character. In the last analysis, that's what schools are for: Character Building. Only character is so hard to teach. You can't give courses in character building; you can't give a boy backbone just by making him go to church. A good example helps, but you can't talk very much about it.
>
> Character, like happiness, is a by-product — a by-product very often of hard work. I do not say that, if a child works hard over a long time, he is sure to strengthen his character. But I do say that it is *likely* to be one result. . .You see, I am old-fashioned and conservative.
>
> By this time you are thinking: "This is all very well to say — that many students do not work hard enough, — but how shall we persuade them to?" That is a hard question. I propose to meet it head on.
>
> I believe that we have too many courses listed in our catalogs. Sir Richard Livingstone says, "The good schoolmaster is known by the number of valuable subjects he declines to teach." I would have our children study fewer subjects, but learn them more thoroughly.
>
> . . . Our whole educational system has become soft. If a child cannot learn Latin, we give him something called Roman Civilization, or perhaps shop work. If he cannot learn Algebra, we give him Business Arithmetic or General Mathematics. Now this is all very well for the child who *cannot* learn Latin or Algebra, but what of the child who simply *does not* learn Latin or Algebra?

He too is given an easier set of courses. If he fails some of these courses, he is promoted just the same, and is eventually graduated. Not only are we failing to educate our boys and girls, but we are actually educating them to low standards of accomplishment.

Such a philosophy has guided the academic program at the Academy from the time the Headmaster took over, but it must not be misunderstood. If the school has depended upon certain traditional concepts, these should not be construed as narrow and inflexible. The development in recent years of such courses as Public Speaking, required of all for graduation; Developmental Reading; advanced English sections in the Great Books; and double courses in English at the ninth and tenth grade levels should immediately dispel any such ideas.

That the boys in the school understood early in the game the purpose of their educational program is suggested by a student editorial in *The Archon* for December, 1934:

> The greatest aid to scholastic, or in fact to any mental work, is concentration. The boy who succeeds, the one who earns the honors, rarely grinds for long hours . . . We say he is bright and does not have to work. The answer is, however, that he works just as hard, but does his school work in much less time because he concentrates. There is no better place than this well supervised school to teach us to concentrate. As soon as we learn that simple lesson, our school work will seem easier, for it takes less time when we waste none of it.

If one were to include in such a history as this the athletic record of a school, the material would exceed all bounds; thus through the years, athletics have been only touched upon. It would be wrong, however, to omit mention of them entirely, for they are an integral and significant part of school life. Particularly has this been true at Governor Dummer under Dr. Eames, for character is built upon the athletic fields as well as in the classrooms and the dormitories. Hard work plays as important a role in football, lacrosse, or tennis as it does in trigonometry; and, in competition, sportsmanship and unselfishness come into play, too. "The normal teen-age boy has an abnormal interest in athletics," the Headmaster would say. "They serve not only to keep him active, but interested as well."

Beginning in the early 'thirties, this belief had a major influence on the structure of the school program. If *every* boy were to have an opportunity to take active part in competition, more facilities had to be provided, more equipment, schedules for younger and less experienced boys as well as for varsity athletes. This belief had a significant bearing, too, on the kind of man who was selected to teach in the school. Men were needed who were not only able instructors, but who liked sports, as well — who would insist on sportsmanlike play, and live it themselves. In the early years Ted Eames himself acted as Athletic Director and coached, at one time or another, most of the major teams. Replacing in 1936 Bill Jacob, who had in previous years turned out some highly successful squads, the Headmaster coached the football team through a wonderful season during which the only loss, by the narrowest of margins, came in the final game, against Moses Brown. On this team played two of the school's all-time stars, fullback Joe Hoague and end Ed Donnelly, both of whom went on to Little All-American honors at Colgate.

Other interesting teams of the 'thirties might well receive mention here. In 1937 Arthur Ross, Jr., son of the owner of Boston's professional Bruins hockey team, led the Governors' skaters to a season which included but one loss. The squad was coached by the Headmaster's brother, Morey Eames (whose sketching classes for several years drew large numbers of Academy boys). The 1931 baseball team, also coached by Ted Eames, is notable particularly for two of its members: catcher John Young, who became a doctor in Maine and later, during the war, was a benefactor of the Academy under most unusual circumstances; and captain and third baseman Howard J. "Buster" Navins, who went on to star in basketball and baseball at Williams College and then in 1936 became the first of the Eames boys to return to Governor Dummer to teach. In 1934 the basketball team, coached by Mr. Reagan, lost a single game, defeating, among others, Phillips Exeter, Phillips Andover, the Harvard Freshmen, and Deerfield.

The year 1936-37 saw, in accordance with Mr. Eames's desire to provide competitive athletics for all of the boys in the school, the establishing of two new team sports: soccer under Mr. Navins, and lacrosse under Mr. Murphy. In the years since then these two coaches, and others, have produced teams in these sports which have been unsurpassed at private schools of comparable size throughout New England, and which have been successful against teams from schools several times the size of Governor Dummer.

During the 'thirties cross country, wrestling, track, tennis, golf, fencing, and skiing also provided boys with opportunities to develop skills and to compete.

There were other interesting diversions available to the boys. Among the most intriguing were the annual Hare and Hounds race and two odysseys to the snow country. In the race, which traditionally started in front of Sunset Hill, nearly every boy in school took part, starting out en masse to follow a rough and intricate trail of paper laid out by two of the older boys. The winning group of boys was rewarded with a Saturday night steak dinner. Mr. Sager must, indeed, have cut a noble figure on that occasion when he set off the chase, dressed in an outfit reminiscent of Robin Hood. Standing silhouetted at the top of Sunset Rock, he signaled the start by sounding a tucket call "with considerable éclat" on a long brass trumpet!

Twice — in March, 1937, and again in 1938 — almost the entire school blithely packed up its cold weather gear and by devious means of transport sallied forth into the snow country for a winter week end. Visualize, if you will, the furrowed brow of logistic expert and wagon master "Mac" Murphy, entrusted with working out the details of transporting and providing for a hundred and a half carefree expedition members. Or picture the Academy's long-time close friend and physician, Dr. Carl Bullard, invited along as a laudable precautionary measure, lightly traversing the snowy slopes — with a handbook on contusions and fractures carefully stuffed into his hip pocket.

But the maddest mix-up of them all has been the "Pushball" pandemonium which has flooded the campus every November since about 1936. Originally intended to occupy the gap between the fall and winter sports seasons, it has become, instead of a mere expedient, a major objective. The entire student body and most of the faculty square off in two leagues of volleyball teams with such alliterative and forbidding titles as Eames's Eagles or Sager's Sharks, and the subsequent civil strife bursts amidst vicious "spikes" and frantic teamwork. Under the aegis of the flamboyant Poobah of Pushball (who never seems quite able to make an actual appearance, but instead leaves matters in the capable hands of his executive emissary, "Uncle Tom" Mercer), the competition burns gloriously until at last the winners in each league have been determined. Then, amidst the vociferous vocalizing of their partisans, the victors vie for their rewards: for the champions, a steak dinner with pie à la mode for dessert; for the runners-up, the steak dinner unadorned.

In such ways as these has the Academy capitalized in recent decades upon its character, not as a large boarding school, but rather, as one where everybody shares with everybody else in whatever is undertaken. Thus spirits have been kept high and the enthusiasm of the boys and the faculty constantly renewed.

On January 15, 1938, a notable event took place, as the Board voted to admit as day students bona fide residents of the Town of Newbury, as well as those from the parish of Byfield, with full scholarships covering all charges of tuition, dependent upon "the usual entrance requirements of scholarship and character." (Exactly one hundred years earlier the Academy's Trustees and Nehemiah Cleaveland had been trying desperately to salvage some good will out of the controversy which had followed the Board's attempt to charge tuition to Byfield scholars.) The action of the 1938 Board was taken "out of respect to the manifest intentions" of the school's founder toward his neighbors. The move was aptly summed up in the February *Archon*:

> . . .Thus the Trustees have marked the 175th year of the school's history with an action adhering closely to the original intention of William Dummer which was to make the school a source of benefit to the community in which it was founded.

The 175th Anniversary of Governor Dummer Academy was not allowed to pass unnoticed. Celebrated at the time of the regular Commencement on June 9 and 10, it attracted more than 1,200 guests to the various exercises. Present with his wife was John Hamilton Morse of the Class of 1885, captain of the Academy's first football team, former Trustee, donor — in fact, architect — of the Morse Athletic Field, and the very man who had been chairman of the committee in charge of the 150th Anniversary celebration in 1913. Present, too, was Dr. Ingham, who in 1913 had addressed those in attendance.

At the 175th, the graduation exercises were opened with a prayer by Mr. Joseph N. Dummer of the class of '76, a Trustee since 1906, already for twenty-six years Secretary of the Board, and a collateral descendant of Governor Dummer.

Seated at the head table during the Commencement Dinner was the Academy's beloved neighbor, a regular at the Vesper services through the year, beekeeper George W. Adams. A member of the class of 1873, the old man once wrote in a letter to the Headmaster (describing the connection between his family and the Academy) that "four generations from this home have been pupils, and of my blood and name there have been two masters [Samuel Adams, 1819-1821; and Frederic Adams, 1840-1846] and two trustees [John Adams, 1792-1804; and Daniel Adams, 1828-1866] with seventy-five enrolled pupils"

A major link between the venerable past and the burgeoning present on this occasion was symbolized by the original Little Red Schoolhouse, newly restored, the work being the gift and the personal concern of the Reverend Glenn Tilley Morse, loyal Trustee and donor of the Morse Flag. On the evening of June 9 Mr. Morse unlocked with a large, old-fashioned key the door of Master Moody's first schoolhouse at the Academy. He then formally presented the key to Mr. Phillips, President of the Board. The restoration, beautifully and faithfully carried out under the direction of William Graves Perry (the same architect who had been charged with the restoration of Williamsburg, Virginia) provided the school from its 175th Anniversary with a thoroughly authentic and appropriate monument to its historic founding in the 18th century and to its venerable past. Today whenever a guest is shown over the Academy, one of the first stops is the Little Red Schoolhouse where it has become a tradition for the guide to toll the bell. Sometimes the bell will clang forth two or three times a day, and the boys in Moody House next door may be heard to say, as boys will, "There she goes again, the largest cash register in the Country" — and the pride in their voices belies the worldliness of their remark. It should not be omitted that among the guests at the formal presentation of the old schoolhouse was Mrs. Sally Moody Cook of York, Maine, the great-great-grandniece of Master Moody himself.

On the following afternoon less formal festivities were celebrated as the talented Governor Dummer baseball team, led by Mr. Eames, defeated its Deerfield rivals, under the guidance of their doughty coach, Dr. Boyden. That evening, performing the duties of toastmaster, Dr. Claude Fuess, Phillips Academy Headmaster and Governor Dummer Trustee, introduced as the main speakers Dr. Karl T. Compton, President of the Massachusetts Institute of Technology; the Reverend James T. Cleland of Amherst College; and James Duncan Phillips.

This historic Commencement was climaxed as Mr. Phillips

traveled back to the early days of the school and skillfully reviewed its growth. Coming up to the present he described the "great ability and constructive skill" which Dr. Ingham devoted to strengthening the Academy. Finally he assessed the accomplishments since 1930:

> Now what have we to show for our stewardship of the last few years. The changes in Perkins and Commons have given us twenty new rooms. Duncan House and the Cottage on the new Campus about as many more. Our new dining hall and its wonderful kitchen have provided for the most serious need of the growing school. Whipple Field with its wonderful possibilities of growth is a magnificent addition. Our physical equipment is rising to meet our needs, very slowly it sometimes seems to your Trustees, but rise it does to meet the crisis every time.

> But back of it all we have the marvelous historical tradition of service to the country, and behind the bricks and the mortar we have a far richer and more valuable asset. I mean the group of earnest faithful men, and let me not forget women, who make up our faculty. I would include everyone from our Headmaster . . . down to the the latest teacher, all are doing their share with character, intelligence, and fidelity to make a great school, not great in size but great in its ability to affect for good the lives and character of its students. Thus at the beginning of the home stretch of the second century of the Academy, we as Trustees are proud to present to you the best equipped, the best manned, and the largest school in the history of the Academy.

It would indeed seem appropriate to end this chapter covering the first eight years of Mr. Eames's headmastership on that last high note — except for one small instance, trivial perhaps, that somehow caps the spirit of growth which pervaded this period. It is recorded in the Headmaster's report to the Trustees at the end of the school year 1938 that "the Headmaster announces with a sigh of relief that an additional small bathroom has been installed for the use of guests on the second floor of the Mansion House"!

CHAPTER XIII

Edward W. Eames

Without question, one of the most important steps that Ted Eames took in his early years at Governor Dummer Academy was to provide himself and the school with a nucleus of gifted teachers around which has grown a strong faculty. In the course of his first seven years, he brought to the Academy eight men who together have set a pattern of high excellence in working with boys. Of the eight, six, who now represent a total of more than 165 years service at the Academy, still comprise the substructure of the Governor Dummer faculty and constitute, without question, the youngest and most active "Old Guard" to be found at any school anywhere!

All of the men have come to play key parts in the life of the school. Two have assumed heavy administrative responsibility. Ed Dunning began as a teacher of English and Mathematics, but his knowledge, training, and resourcefulness soon found him working as Registrar and finally carrying out the multifarious duties of Business Manager. Patient but firm, goodhumored but forthright, he has commanded the respect and cooperation of generations of boys. Ben Stone — since 1932 a gifted teacher at the Academy, for years head of the Mathematics Department, Registrar, Director of Admissions, and finally Director of Studies — has been aptly described by Mr. Eames as "a good team player." Tireless yet unassuming, demanding yet understanding, he has at one time or another borne active responsibility in practically every aspect of the life of the school.

Former Olympic athlete (whose familiar title is "The Bull") Art Sager is an inexhaustible reservoir of energy and enthusiasm. Dynamic and versatile, with a genuine concern for boys, he possesses the invaluable knack of teaching by showing. One of his finest contributions has been his work to help establish and maintain continuing good will with alumni and friends of the Academy. Upon these three men, Ed Dunning, Ben Stone, and Art Sager, devolved the responsibility of administering the school during Mr. Eames's leave of absence in 1950. As an Executive Committee they acted with exceptional skill and judgment.

138

Two of the three remaining members of the "Old Guard" still at the school have from the start provided the English Department with a challenging and highly successful program. Head of the Department from the outset, Tom Mercer combines with the true warmth of the Kentuckian a trenchant wit and a genius for teaching boys. A scholar as well as a gentleman, his imaginative and alert management of the English curriculum has made it one of the strong points in the Governor Dummer training. "Uncle Tom's" colleague, Mac Murphy, is learned, patient and, most of all, gentle in his dealings with people. Added to these, he is a fine athlete and coach, an expert woodsman — and a demanding instructor in the classroom. Out of a fundamental respect for all that may be good in each individual whom he meets comes his rare gift for teaching.

The sixth member of the team came to Governor Dummer with the first of them, but as a student, not a teacher. "I attended GDA for only one year before going to college," says Buster Navins, "and I was so impressed with every aspect of the school and its environment that right then and there I decided that some day I would like to return and become a part of it." Return he did, in 1936. With a contagious enthusiasm for life, an infinite capacity for friendship, he has taught his boys, on and off the athletic field, to be keen competitors, to win graciously, and to lose with dignity and control.

These men and their wives, together with the Headmaster and Mrs. Eames, have played the major part in establishing a right atmosphere at Governor Dummer Academy. Each has, in his own way, been particularly successful in helping boys to respect others and to value and develop their own characters and their own talents. Each man possesses an integrity and a fundamental generosity which have won him the respect and affection of hundreds of young men.

Through the years other gifted teachers have come to Governor Dummer. Some of them have been young men just beginning their teaching; some have brought with them a wealth of experience. Some have stayed a year, or a few years, and have moved on; some of the best, like French teacher Roy A. Ohrn, who joined the faculty in 1941, have stayed on and added strength to an already strong group.

They cannot all be named here. There are two men, however, who must not go without mention. William B. Jacob, instructor in Latin, coach of football, and from 1933 to 1938 Assistant Headmaster; and Philip H. Cobb, instructor in Biology and coach of younger boys — these two men died tragically within twelve days of one another in November of 1938. Their deaths were a deep — and deeply felt — loss to the Academy, and came at the end of a twelve month period in the course of which the school had suffered the loss by death of four valued friends.

In the fall of the preceding year the Reverend Carroll Perry, a Trustee of the School for seven years and rector of the Ascension Memorial Church of Ipswich (attended regularly by many of the masters and boys) had died. Brother of famous brothers — Professor-Emeritus Bliss Perry of Harvard, and Dr. Lewis Perry, Headmaster of Phillips Exeter Academy — Carroll Perry through his vitality, wit and loyalty to the Academy was looked upon by all as a valued friend.

Then, in January, 1938, Carrie G. Knight Ambrose, graduate of the Academy in 1876 (when she won the Moody Kent prize for general excellence) passed away. For twenty-two years she had been Postmistress in the South Byfield Post Office, which was in her home just up the road from the Academy. For twenty-seven years previous to that she had assisted the Postmaster, her husband, Frank M. Ambrose, himself a graduate of the school in the 'seventies. A neighbor of the Academy all her life, she probably had known more boys at Governor Dummer than any other person. *The Milestone* dedication to her in 1936, on the sixtieth anniversary of her graduation, pointed out that it was for her that many visiting alumni inquired first.

Following hard upon the loss of two such old friends of the school as Reverend Perry and Mrs. Ambrose, the almost simultaneous deaths of two of the most respected members of the faculty came as a severe shock to all. Bill Jacob, slight of stature, but big of heart and spirit, had thrown himself into his coaching, his teaching, all of his associations with boys with an intensity which drew equal response from those with whom he worked. His standards in everything he did — whether in class or in the woods (for he was an ardent woodsman) — were rigorous; but whatever he demanded of others, he lived up to himself. One who taught at Governor Dummer with him describes him as "a man whose deep devotion was to boys, a man who set them an example of the unwearied pursuit of perfection rather than adequacy. . ."

To capture the spirit of Philip H. Cobb in a brief paragraph, or to attempt to reflect his profound influence in the school — indeed, on virtually everyone who knew him— seems unattainable. Rising completely above his physical handicap, he was an example of simple, thorough goodness. He loved other people and was kind. President Sills of Bowdoin said of him:

> . . .his boys not only respected him, they loved him, and love based on respect is among the very finest of human emotions.

In Moody House he could be on his knees wrestling with his young charges ten minutes before "lights out." At "lights out" there would be absolute order and quiet. The boys wanted to do what he wanted them to do. One of his colleagues says of him: "Phil Cobb was the best boys' man I have ever known."

Ted Eames has built in many ways, but nowhere has he built better than in the staff of his school.

* * * * *

The excellence of the faculty has affected the school program in many areas, but most significantly at its core, the academic program. At this "old-fashioned New England school" the emphasis has continued to rest heavily upon the traditional disciplines in the areas of English, Mathematics, the sciences (notably biology, chemistry, and physics) and foreign languages (including Latin). Over the years the curriculum has remained essentially flexible, so that constructive additions and revisions have intensified its effectiveness, but fundamentally the program has changed little. Its purpose has remained to train boys to work hard, to think and to act effectively. The goal to which it has led most boys has been college. Over the first ten years of Mr. Eames's administration at Governor Dummer, 401 graduates of the Academy entered college. For the years 1931-1940 inclusive, the distribution of graduates among the colleges was as follows:

Colleges Requiring College Board Examinations		Other Colleges	
Harvard University	33 boys	Bowdoin College	37 boys
Massachusetts Institute of Technology	13	Williams College	37
		Amherst College	35
Princeton University	7	Dartmouth College	33
Yale University	6	Brown University	19
		University of Maine	11
		Middlebury College	11
		Worcester Polytechnic Institute	11
		Colgate University	10
		Colleges with ten or fewer boys	138

As early as 1934 the Academy had been elected to membership in the Cum Laude Society, the purpose of which is to encourage and reward high academic attainment by secondary school students. Those designated as faculty-members immediately adopted by-laws and formally established the Governor Dummer Chapter.

Provisions were made to keep in touch with graduates of the Academy. Mr. Eames, members of the faculty, and selected students attended informal receptions and luncheons from time to time at colleges where numbers of Governor Dummer boys were continuing their studies. An interesting sidelight from this period, connected with alumni relations, is the fact that at Commencement time in 1939 by vote of the Trustees Miss Carrie S. Dummer was awarded a certificate of graduation as of 1879. Miss Dummer, sister of Secretary of the Board Joseph N. Dummer, had been a student at the Academy when girls were admitted during the administration of Eben Parsons. The certificate was, as she described it in her note of thanks, "a bright cloud in the sunset of life."

Meanwhile the school was continuing its steady expansion. The generosity of Mrs. Carrie Ambrose and other friends of the school had made it possible for the Trustees to acquire Ambrose House, formerly Mrs. Ambrose's home and the location of the South Byfield Post Office. Older than even the Mansion House (part of the building dates from about 1695), this fine old Colonial home, built on a section of the original Richard Dummer grant, was extensively remodeled to provide space for a married master's apartment and ten students.

It was while visiting in the new apartment at Ambrose House that Mr. Benjamin Pearson, graduate and neighbor of the school, heard from a member of the faculty that there had been certain complaints about Academy students swimming in the Parker River from land not belonging to the school. Shortly afterward Mr. Pearson gave to the Academy four acres of salt marsh property southwest of ancient Thurlow's Bridge over the Parker.

The original impetus toward providing the New Building for the school had come from the boys; as a result, the kitchen and dining room wing had reached completion in the autumn of 1936. Early in 1939 a group of students once more took the initiative. Recognizing the need for completing the project, they first approached Mr. Murphy of the faculty and then late in November called a meeting to lay their suggestions before Mr. Eames and the entire school. Before the Christmas holidays they were assured of the enthusiastic support of the Trustees. By June the drive which the boys had initiated had gone over the top.

The goal was accomplished in spite of what might seem a serious set-back. Early in 1940 the main classroom building on the campus caught fire. As reported in the February *Archon:*

> The Parsons Schoolhouse was badly gutted by flames on the night of January 24 and was reduced to a total loss [sic]. Breaking out about 9 o'clock in the rear wall of the 2½-story building as a result of a defective chimney, the fire rapidly gained headway as it ate its way in the partitions of the walls, and the combined efforts of the Newburyport, Rowley and Byfield fire departments were necessary to bring the flames under control after a two hour battle . . .

Many of the irreplaceable records from the school business office (Mr. Eames's office was still in the Mansion House) and much of the scientific apparatus from the laboratory were carried to safety by older boys under the supervision of masters. The firemen, handicapped by bitter cold which froze the water from the hoses almost as soon as it hit the building, did well to prevent the school-house from burning to the ground. An emergency meeting of the faculty, called by Mr. Eames as soon as the fire was under control, quickly produced an effective "crash program" for continuing classes. Certain school offices were moved temporarily into the Little Red Schoolhouse. Newburyport High School came forth with a generous offer of their new chemistry laboratory for science classes.

The fact remained, however, that in the midst of a campaign to complete the New Building, Parsons Schoolhouse had to be rebuilt. The shell remained, and it was decided to retain the original exterior, with two minor changes. The entire interior had to be restored, however. By careful management of the insurance money, Mr. Eames and the Board made effective provision without jeopardizing their new plans. The Schoolhouse, still retaining much of the original framework upon which it had been constructed 120 years earlier, was rebuilt and newly equipped, ready for use at the opening of school in the fall of 1940.

One intriguing episode arising from the Parsons fire deserves mention. It was reported by the Headmaster to the Trustees at their June meeting:

> In recognition of their services, the Academy invited the forty-five firemen who fought the blaze to a dinner a few days after the fire. . .

It was added that the guests were entertained by the Academy Glee Club — and that, of the forty-five who were invited, *fifty-five* appreciative "firemen" actually attended the festivities.

During the summer the contract for completion of the New Building was awarded and work begun. Alumni Day, May 17, 1941, celebrated the official opening of the entire building. Containing, in addition to the dining hall and kitchen already in use, a large reception hall and a school living room suitable for evening meetings and vesper services, it filled a crucial and long-felt need at the Academy. Besides the facilities already mentioned, there were on the first two floors offices for Mr. Eames and his administrative staff, a school post office and store giving onto an informal lounge for the boys. On the upper floors were a small faculty apartment, single rooms for nine boys, and two large general purpose rooms (since remodeled into accommodations for six more boarding students). Thus with recent increases in boarding facilities at Duncan House, the Cottage, Ambrose House, and the New Building, Governor Dummer was able to open the 1941-1942 school year with its largest enrollment in history: 154 boys, including 123 boarders. In ten years its enrollment had doubled.

Three months later the Japanese attacked Pearl Harbor. Immediately the Academy was brought into a position of preparedness. With most of the members of the Byfield Volunteer Fire Department drafted into the service or away during the day in defense work, a Governor Dummer fire brigade — two companies of two masters and twenty boys each — was formed and trained to cover any fire calls in the parish between the hours of seven A. M. and seven P. M. Mr. Eames, who was to become an enthusiastic aficionado of fire fighting, purchased the first item in his soon-to-grow collection of old hand pumpers, the "Red Wing" from Salisbury, and loaned it to the fire brigade for use at the school. Blackout precautions were taken and an air raid warden system was set up. Faculty wives became very active in defense, Red Cross, and relief work.

THE JAMES DUNCAN PHILLIPS BUILDING

A POPULAR CORNER OF THE COBB ROOM

Up to now Governor Dummer men had played significant roles in every war in this nation's history. Now the impact of world conflict made itself felt at the school, as it did everywhere else. Once again, as months passed, younger faculty members, members of the Academy's maintenance crew, and even older boys were called into service. The actual program of the school, however, with everyone pitching in to help, proceeded with a minimum of change. The boys took over responsibility for much of the upkeep in the dormitories and elsewhere on campus. Following meals in the school dining halls, faculty wives helped to reset the tables. Athletic schedules at all levels in the school underwent little curtailment (though modes of travel to away games included, according to certain of the coaches, everything except the Overland Stage). It was strongly felt that most of the activities at Governor Dummer, if they had been soundly based in the first place, were doubly important to the training of young men in a time of war.

Mr. Eames explained the school's policy in a vigorous letter to parents and students:

> . . . Those boys who sincerely wish to contribute as much as they possibly can toward winning the war ought, not only to continue with their education as long as they can, but also to *intensify* their training . . . I believe it is our duty to help each boy train his mind, toughen his body, and strengthen his character. Insofar as we succeed in doing these things, we shall be preparing our boys for war service, and incidentally for college.

> Now I submit that this is exactly the sort of job the good preparatory schools have been doing for many years. . . We have always thought that character, built on hard work and hard play, was the first goal of any good school. . .The basic and established policy of the school remains unchanged. . .

Since the government had recently requested that secondary schools everywhere offer pre-flight aviation training, the Academy instituted special courses in navigation, meteorology, and mathematics. A few other minor changes in the school program were made. Participation in contact sports was required of all boys except those with physical disabilities. "I believe that an athletic program, properly administered, helps rather than hinders most boys' studies," wrote Mr. Eames. "I believe, too, that this program of 'athletics for all' is one of the most important features of schools like Governor

Dummer — and never more important than at the present time." In the spirit of these statements the Academy continued to function effectively.

Throughout these years the remarkable letters written monthly by the Headmaster (beginning at Christmastime, in 1942) constituted inspired, and perhaps unique, contributions to the spirit and morale of Governor Dummer graduates around the world. For some time before he wrote his first letter, Mr. Eames had been receiving communications from Governor Dummer men in every corner of the United States and every quarter of the globe. Many of them sounded the same note: a hint of loneliness, a longing to hold on to familiar recollections, and to cling to old friendships.

The second letter in the series set the pattern for those to follow. There was news of the school and of its personnel. There were lists of addresses of the widely scattered alumni. Particularly, there was news of the activities of the graduates, excerpted from their letters: their memories of the school and of one another, their experiences in training, their adventures in the theatres of war, their tragedies, their deaths, their heroism. The response was overwhelming. Great numbers of communications reached the school from all over the world, filled with reports, many of them movingly expressed, of thoughts and acts, of hardships lived through, of courage displayed — and especially of gratitude for the newsletters. "I shall be writing again next month," promised the Headmaster, "and each month thereafter until the war is won. You may depend on that."

To read the letters is to experience with a striking sense of realism the anguish of war and its concomitant glories and sacrifices. There are included excerpts from letters from Tulagi, from Guadalcanal, England, Italy, Tunisia, India, New Guinea — the world around. Sometimes the newsletters enclosed a photograph of a Governor Dummer faculty member and his family, or of a familiar campus scene. On rare occasions Mrs. Eames or a member of the "Old Guard" stepped in for the Headmaster to compose the monthly letter.

A smattering of the responses can but suggest their dramatic qualities:

> I have lost a number of my closest friends and have heard Gabriel take a breath to blow his horn on several occasions.

Bathing in the jungle is difficult since water must be carried long distances. I find I can shave, bathe and wash all my clothes — and rinse them — in two quarts of water.

"I can't tell you how much your monthly letter means to me. The boys sure are doing O. K., aren't they?" commented a fighter pilot in England. And from a G. I.:

I hope you can read this okay. I'm not so hot at writing — no reflections on Gov. Dummer. It's just the foxhole is cramped and my hand is a little shaky. My best to all the faculty and also to Mrs. Eames and the family.

An impressive number of men recalled with appreciation the vesper services at school. From the Philippines:

It sure is a long way from the vesper service I sat at seven years ago tonight, but it isn't hard to remember. Even now in the midst of all this mess over here I can still hear the singing . . . I don't think I ever really knew just how much my lone year at Governor Dummer meant to me. Sometimes in the flashbacks you have in times of danger, some one thing will be evident. My wife and son are always first, of course, but a number of times, a clear picture of events at the school came in front of me and brought me to realize what a permanent impression it had left. Consider my son an applicant for admission about 1960.

From somewhere in the Pacific a former Morse Flag winner wrote:

I, as you know, was a little late getting into this fracas, but I believe I am slowly making up for it. I was in the Leyte and Lingayen Gulf invasions; that's all I can say. War is just like the old ball game; nervous as hell (or whatever that feeling is at the bottom of your stomach), but as soon as the action starts, back to normal you go. Takes the fun out of it, though, when the opponent has no standards of fair play, and you know the game is for keeps.

It is not hard to imagine how much the newsletters — telling such stories as that concerning former baseball catcher Dr. John

Young's remarkable wartime gift to the Academy, or concerning the astounding escape of ex-hockey Captain Art Ross, Jr., from occupied France — must have meant to hundreds of Governor Dummer graduates or how much their responses meant to those back at the school.

News of the end of the war came on the Headmaster's birthday, which the Eameses were celebrating by having their and the school's good friends Dr. and Mrs. Bullard to dinner. Mr. Eames's report of the Doctor's excitement on V-J Day is worth quoting:

> The Doctor obviously wanted to let off steam, and we soon had him tugging on the bell rope in the Old Red Schoolhouse. This brought Nan and Neddy Stone the children of Mr. and Mrs. Ben Stone of the faculty out of Moody House on the run. They hopped up and down, their eyes growing bigger and brighter, and soon they were helping Dr. Bullard with the rope.

The Academy had weathered the war years well. The school had remained full, and though younger teachers had of necessity come and gone, the hard core of experienced faculty members was enabled to stay on. A small nucleus of key maintenance personnel stood by; the boys helped with the work. It is interesting that during two of the most difficult years welcome assistance was rendered by William D. Sprague, popular teacher under Perley Horne and himself Headmaster for two years back in 1904-1906, who, though retired after many years as a public school administrator, returned to the Academy to assist with supervision and instruction.

During the war, for "those boys who had made good records and had not been able to complete their studies at the Academy owing to the requirements of military service," special wartime diplomas had been awarded:

> An unusual feature of the Graduation exercises on Saturday morning, Commencement, 1944, was the awarding of both regular and special diplomas to boys who had been compelled, because of their age, to enter military service before the close of the school year. Most of these diplomas were awarded in absentia and it was a moving sight when mothers and fathers came down the aisle to receive a diploma from Mr. Phillips's hand. In one instance, a boy's young and attractive sister came forward to receive his diploma and when she appeared

THE CHARLES S. INGHAM HOUSE

in front of the senior class, the applause rose to new heights.

As part of this same Commencement, the New Building was dedicated as the James Duncan Phillips Building, in honor of the President of the Board of Trustees since 1932.

Early in 1944 the Trustees had voted to Mr. Eames special authorization to proceed in working out long range plans "for the development of the school, its student body, its faculty, its buildings and equipment." Assured now of the soundness of the school's condition, the Board could anticipate its further growth. The first evidences were not long in making their appearance. By November of 1944, a new brick wing had been built onto the venerable Perkins Dormitory, providing accommodations for nineteen additional students. The Academy opened that fall with an enrollment of 174 boys. About the time that the new wing was opened, formal announcement was made of a new brick dormitory to be built on Broadback Hill and to be named in honor of former Headmaster Charles S. Ingham. The building was planned to contain single rooms for thirty-nine older boys and two unmarried masters. In addition, a two-story dwelling for a married master was incorporated in the design. Ground was broken immediately. When the dedication ceremonies were held two years later, on May 30, Dr. Ingham was present to give his interesting and highly entertaining dedication address.

As the school grew it became increasingly clear that the Lang Gymnasium could not by itself provide adequate facilities for the busy athletic program. At the same time, there was a strong feeling among the faculty that some memorial should be established to those hundreds of alumni who were serving their country in the Second World War. The two needs were incorporated, and a campaign was initiated to raise funds for a Memorial Gymnasium. With members of the faculty very active in fund-raising, over $70,000 had been received in cash and pledges by February, 1945, when a special issue of *The Archon* was printed, outlining the project. A brief quotation from this issue will serve both to establish the significance of the new plans and to emphasize the practical wisdom underlying the general growth of the school.

A new building, even a prospective new building, is a milestone in the life of any school. And a milestone, by custom, is an appropriate place to pause for a survey of the road that has been already traversed. . .Surveying the fifteen years of Mr. Eames's stewardship from the vantage point of a new project brings a sense of solid accomplishment. . .But first things have come first. The student body has been increased slowly and with discrimination. The records of the graduates, whether in college or in the armed forces, has been highly honorable. The physical plant has grown steadily rather than sensationally. Each acquisition has come only when the need for it was imperative. The road from 1930 has been through difficult times and places, but the milestones stand firm and enduring. May the new gymnasium be one of the proudest!

1945 stood out as a personal milestone for Ted Eames, too. His school was thriving. He himself was serving as President of the New England Association of Colleges and Secondary Schools. At Commencement time in a surprise ceremony, Trustees, faculty, students and friends paid tribute to him, as well as to Mrs. Eames, on his fifteenth anniversary as Headmaster. His college, Amherst, honored him by electing him to serve a six-year term as an alumni trustee. Bowdoin College, at her Sesquicentennial Exercises a year earlier, had conferred upon him the honorary degree of Doctor of Humane Letters. Concerning Ted Eames, the words of Dr. Fuess at the June Commencement serve simply and well to sum up the case: "His fifteen years in this spot have been good for him and good for Governor Dummer — indeed for all of us present."

CHAPTER XIV

Edward W. Eames

The next two years at Governor Dummer Academy provided ample evidence that the recent pattern of expansion and growth — not only academically, as will become abundantly clear, but also physically — was to continue at a steady pace in the post-war era. In these two years the results of long-range planning initiated in 1944 began to manifest themselves.

The purchase during the summer of 1945 of "Boynton Meadow," about sixteen acres of property bordering Morse Field to the north, provided land for the soon-to-be-built Alumni Gymnasium (and, in later years, for a much-needed new athletic field and track). At the same time, work was well under way on Ingham House, slated for occupancy in the fall of '46.

At the Trustees' meeting in September of 1945 it was announced that the Gymnasium Fund drive for $125,000 had gone over the top. With building costs spiraling, however, it was decided to postpone construction until a careful assessment of the new circumstances could be made and appropriate adjustments planned.

Nevertheless, needed additions continued to be made in careful stages. For example, by the fall of 1947 the Farmhouse on the old Noyes property had been remodeled to provide accommodations for the Academy steward and his family, the chef, and a dozen to fourteen additional members of the commissary and housekeeping departments. The following spring ground was broken for a wing to Peirce Hall, whereby a much-needed faculty apartment would be gained, as well as additional rooms for several boys. With the new space here and in Ingham House, there would now be accommodations for over 190 boarding students.

With all the evidence of judicious expansion and in spite of the successful fund-raising for a new gymnasium (spearheaded by Mr. Philip Morgan for the Trustees and Art Sager, aided by Buster Navins, of the faculty), it began to look as though the building program might bog down in a morass of rising prices. This, even in the face of the first in a series of remarkable gifts from a single deeply interested alumnus. Requesting that for the time being he remain anonymous, this benefactor had expressed a desire to underwrite the entire cost of a magnificent new classroom and science building, including all contents and furnishings, as well as the landscaping. By its very nature this gift, announced at the Commencement Dinner in May, 1946, symbolized the respect and confidence which months and years of painstaking planning under Dr. Eames had won for Governor Dummer Academy.

Just when the problem of cost threatened an end to any hope of further building, however, the alumnus-donor once again demonstrated his understanding and his desire to help the school. Subordinating his own wishes to the immediate needs, he agreed to deferment of plans for the classroom building and added his generous contribution to the fund for the gymnasium.

Today the Alumni Gymnasium, completed in the spring of 1950, stands as clear evidence of meticulous planning by the Headmaster and his advisors. The first building of modern design on the campus, it, nonetheless, fits attractively into the setting; and, both in its light-colored brick outer construction and its capacious tiled interior, it provides excellent and efficient facilities for a wide variety of activities, not exclusively athletic. The first fortunate boys to enjoy these facilities were the seniors of the Class of 1950, who moved into the locker rooms in the spring of that year. Then, on June 3, Admiral William F. "Bull" Halsey, famed leader of the Allied naval forces in the South Pacific in World War II, presented the dedication address to a Commencement audience of over 1,350 people. Beneath the Dedicatory Plaque in the Memorial Lobby, on a built-in, glass-covered table, an engrossed parchment lists the names of all alumni of the Academy who had served in the war, with a special section devoted to those who had given their lives.

High enthusiasm for the Academy had sprung up among those who had been witness to its growth in size and vitality. Such tangible gifts as the two greatly appreciated all-weather tennis courts constructed near Whipple Field in the spring of '49 (two others have since been added, bringing the total at the school to six) demonstrate that parents and friends were taking a continuing interest. Yet despite the evident enthusiasm, Governor Dummer found itself with very nearly the lowest endowment among the good private secondary schools of the East. She deserved better. Closer liaison with her friends was needed.

Since the end of the school year of 1941 a new alumni body had been quietly building. For years the old association, the Sons of

THE ALUMNI GYMNASIUM

Dummer, which had intermittently for over 100 years been a source of support for the school, had lain dormant. Kept alive only by that crusty, but staunch and long-time supporter of the Academy, John Hamilton Morse, it passed away when in the spring of 1945 he established with its remaining resources a fund for the purchase of books for the library.

In September of 1946, the new alumni group announced the establishment of the "1763" Fund (in 1957 redesignated the *Governor Dummer Alumni Fund*), intended as an annual gift from the alumni to the school. Communication between the Academy and its alumni continued to improve. The spring of 1947 brought forth the first annual *Alumni Bulletin*. In it Dr. Eames's letter to the graduates closed with the following paragraph:

> This has been a remarkable year for alumni activity. For the first time in many years, dinners have been held both in Boston and in New York. The 1763 Fund is off to a fine start. The first issue of the Alumni Bulletin has been published. We now look forward to an Alumni Day in May and to the dedication of Ingham House at Commencement time. I hope we may welcome back to school more and more of the older boys from all parts of the country on these two occasions, and indeed on any occasion at all.

Strengthening of relations with the alumni did not stop at this point. Shortly afterward the Trustees voted to invite two members of the Alumni Association to sit with the Board for the period of one year. The policy was greeted with enthusiasm and has been continued with great success and mutual benefit ever since. From it the Trust has not only reaped annually the advantage of strong support and welcome comment, but also, on more than one occasion, of strong addition to its own permanent membership. The first alumni representative to be elected to the Board was, in 1949, Roger B. Coulter, a leading Boston trial lawyer who in 1913 had been winner of the first Morse Flag award and whose own son had graduated from the Academy just a few weeks before his father's election as a trustee.

At the same time that the alumni began to lend increasing strength to the school, closer contact with parents and friends was being fostered as well. The first annual Parents' Day, on October 18, 1948, was an unqualified success and gave vivid proof of the desire of parents and friends to share in the life of the Academy.

Over 300 guests enjoyed the day on campus, including the dinner in their honor. The boys, in the spirit of the occasion, delighted the visitors by coming through unscathed against strong opposition on the athletic fields: 4 to 2 in varsity soccer, and 26 to 0 in varsity football. Parents' Day had immediately become a popular and well attended fixture.

The life of the school continued, as it had for many years, to revolve around the familiar goal for its boys: "Character built on hard work and hard play." The broad athletic program, geared to boys of all sizes, ages, and degrees of proficiency, remained central to this philosophy, as amply evidenced each fall, when four football squads (Varsity, "C" squad, "Lightning," and "Pony") and three soccer squads (Varsity, Junior Varsity, and "Pony") played outside schedules.

Through the years there have been many thrilling games and many memorable teams — not all of them undefeated. No one who was a witness will forget the heart-stopping tactics of the 1949 basketball team, spearheaded by five boys who worked together with almost instinctive precision, climaxed by the winning of the Class "B" Championship at the Massachusetts Preparatory School Tournament in Boston. Yet even of those teams which prevailed through an entire season without a loss, there is space to mention but a portion, and then only in passing. The 1952 football team, undefeated in seven games, not only rolled up 148 points to 56 for its opponents, but also sent some of its members on to become outstanding college football players. The wrestlers, a closely knit and fiercely competitive squad year in and year out, compiled remarkable records on the way to undefeated seasons in 1952, 1957, and again in 1959.

Sparked by a generous handful of leaders, including "Shad" Tubman and Fulton Yancy, son and nephew respectively of President William Tubman of Liberia, the 1953 soccer team (only one of the several brilliant GDA soccer squads of the last fifteen years) outscored its opponents at the rate of eight goals to one in sweeping undefeated to the Private School League championship. Early in 1956 the lacrosse team defeated Andover for the third year running, and from there marched spectacularly through eight more victories to their first unbeaten season. In 1956 and 1957 the spring track teams were undefeated in dual meets and won the Class "B" title at the Andover Interscholastic meets for the third and fourth times in four years.

In no sense, however, has the school life outside of the class-room centered primarily on the athletic field. Some of the same boys who sparked the 1949 basketball champions played outstanding roles in the 1950 Glee Club and its fine augmented double quartet, the Meistersingers. It was this Glee Club which shared with the choruses from six other preparatory schools (Beaver Country Day School, Dana Hall, Walnut Hill, and Milton, Exeter, and Andover Academies) — a total of 320 voices — in a remarkable concert performed at Symphony Hall in Boston. Fostered by Art Sager as President of the New England Preparatory School Festival Chorus, it was under the baton of Mr. Wilfred Pelletier, Senior Conductor of the Metropolitan Opera Association, and was accompanied by fifty members of the Boston Symphony Orchestra. The 320 young people presented the Bach *Magnificat* and Fauré's *Requiem Mass*, such a program as later drew from one noted Boston music critic the following accolade: "Judged from the severest professional standards, the concert was no less than extraordinary; judged by school standards it was — I deplore the use of the word but none other quite fits — terrific."

These annual concerts, experiences of rare value for the young men and women, now cap the climax of each active year of music and arouse the admiration and enthusiam of all those connected with them. Asked after the 1950 program whether he would be willing to conduct again, Mr. Pelletier told Mr. Sager, "I would not only like to do so, but I would consider it an honor."

Through such other outlets as the Radio Club, the Rifle Club, the Debating Club and the Camera Club, the boys' interests have found expression down through the years. In the late 'forties a Religious Discussion Group developed from the earnest request of both boys and members of the faculty. In more recent years the Senior Council has taken increasing responsibility for the direction of various aspects of school life. These, together with work on the boards of *The Archon* or of *The Milestone*, illustrate some of the organized and productive activities in which the boys have part.

From the many aspects of school life already touched upon, and from others not mentioned, this writer is confronted with a host of memories stemming from three pleasant and valuable years spent as a member of the Governor Dummer faculty at the end of the 'forties: the awesome recollection for example, of occupying — as a fledgling teacher and for one glorious hour each day — the hallowed seat of "Uncle Tom" Mercer at the head of the great oblong table in Noyes Library (leading a class in English 4 during one of the great man's free periods). Nor can anything erase the aching memory of trying to coach a hockey team during the winter of 1948. Over 100 inches of snow fell in Newburyport that winter, most of it, we were convinced, cascading onto our two ice rinks. Each man and boy must have scraped and shoveled away tons of snow; by mid-season the accumulated drifts at rinkside were twice the height of the tallest of us.

Today I can never watch an inside reverse executed on a football field without stirring the vivid Parents' Day recollection of one of the smallest Pony "scatbacks" (so small that he could scarcely be discerned from across the line of scrimmage) scuttling undetected through a quick-opening hole into the enemy end zone— at the very moment that his delighted parents walked onto the field. (This play was the secret weapon of the Ponies during a season when the smallest boys in school compiled an awesome array of victories.)

In the spring of 1949 the grand-daddy of all South Byfield base-ball games saw the Governors play to a taut-nerved fifteen inning stalemate with Kimball Union Academy. Every spectator and participant hung on each crackling pitch; and even at the end of the marathon not a thought had been given by any of us to our long-postponed suppers — or the neglected homework assign-ments.

In the years after the war, however, it was the academic program of the Academy, aimed as always at motivating and enabling boys to work, think, and act effectively, that continued to occupy the center of school life. Basically it retained its emphasis upon the traditional pattern of intensive preparation for college, focusing upon English composition and literature, mathematics and the sciences, history, and foreign languages. Small classes, averaging thirteen to fourteen students, permitted the challenging give-and-take of discussions as well as periodic individual conferences with the teachers.

Whenever change offered promise of progress, however, it was implemented. By 1947 a half-credit course in Public Speaking had become a unique and valuable requirement for all seniors. This addition was but the first step toward meeting the increased pressure for sharpened communications skills. In order to stand up more effectively to this pressure the whole English curriculum at the Academy has in recent years undergone careful readjustment.

It began with the tantalizing "Mercergrams," vocabulary "brain-busters" which weekly during the last years of the 'forties took the measure of students and faculty alike. Later the English department expanded its language program to include for about three-quarters of the boys at the ninth grade level, and in addition to their normal course, a program in *Language Study* to provide further training in composition, vocabulary, spelling, reading, and précis-writing. For sophomores the regular course in English 2 was supplemented by a required half-unit course which, employing among other devices specially prepared reading films, has fostered remarkable achievement in developmental reading and vocabulary.

For advanced seniors in English, assignment to a special class basing its study upon "The Great Books" became a coveted goal. Such changes as these were calculated to meet stiffening requirements for success in college and in a society growing rapidly more complex.

In personnel, in the decade and a half after World War II, Governor Dummer Academy waxed strong and sturdy. The active and able "Old Guard" of the faculty found itself continually strengthened by the addition of intelligent and capable young teachers. Still, there was clear truth in the statement made by Director of Admissions John Witherspoon in the 1957 issue of the *Alumni Bulletin:*

> No matter how fine the plant or how strong the faculty, no school can be better than its boys, for the boys learn as much from each other as they do from the faculty. . .

In this respect, too, the Academy and its boys have in late years shared particularly good fortune. By 1957 the school was receiving inquiries from ten boys for every student that it could accept. Each new boy in school had emerged successful where four others, often strong applicants in their own rights, had to be turned away.

Certain facts compiled in 1959 serve to underscore the strength achieved in the student body. In relation to the nation-wide averages attained on the Achievement Tests of the College Entrance Examination Board, Governor Dummer seniors compiled over a period of five years (1955-1959) the following record:

	No. of GDA Students Involved	National Averages Published by CEEB	Average GDA Score
English Composition	132	527	585
Social Studies	66	523	576
Advanced Mathematics	71	606	637
Physics	32	537	598
French	66	524	599*
Spanish	47	488	543*

*Note: French and Spanish scores have been adjusted upward and downward according to the number of years of training.

In addition, in the same five-year period average scores of Governor Dummer seniors on the Verbal and the Mathematics sections of the Scholastic Aptitude Test climbed steadily, reaching total gains of 40 and 47 points respectively. In the ten-year period from the fall of 1949 through the fall of 1958, 615 graduates of the Academy (out of 631), gained admission to the following colleges and universities:

Harvard	67 boys
Amherst	46
Brown	42
Dartmouth	38
Princeton	30
Colby	24
Yale	23
University of New Hampshire	21
Trinity	20
Washington and Lee	18
Bowdoin	17
Cornell	15
Middlebury	15
Williams	13
Hamilton	12
Kenyon	10
University of Virginia	10
Other Colleges (70)	194
	615 boys

Following Commencement:
The graduates break away from the Mansion House lawn

THE MORRIS PRATT FROST LIBRARY AND SCIENCE BUILDING

THE NEW LIBRARY: INTERIOR

As a college preparatory boarding school for boys, Governor Dummer Academy had attained an indisputably strong position. As a privately endowed institution, she had likewise moved onto a very much stronger footing. With the establishment of the 1763 Fund in 1946, a means of giving was provided the alumni, which has led to significant gifts to Academy funds. For the year 1959, nearly 400 alumni contributed over $14,000 through the Governor Dummer Alumni Fund, an important reflection of wide interest in the school. Throughout the early '50's year-end gifts by other friends of the school grew until they amounted to almost $21,000 for the year 1954. The monetary support was deeply appreciated; still more important as a welcome source of encouragement was the evidence it gave of the Academy's standing in the eyes of its growing numbers of enthusiasts.

In January of 1954 the Trustees received word of the largest gift which had ever been made to Governor Dummer Academy solely for the purpose of endowment. Miss Zella M. Williams of New York, a friend and a relative of the Eames family, had died just after Christmas. Her will provided for the establishing of a fund designated as the Edward Williams Eames Fund, "in honor of her cousin, Edward W. Eames, the present Headmaster of Governor Dummer Academy." The net income of the fund was to be used for the general purposes of the Academy. The amount realized from the bequest has been about $250,000. It is difficult to express adequately the significance of such a gift to a school which in 1930 could lay claim to the most slender of endowment funds.

Beginning in 1938 with a first gift (toward the construction of the Phillips Building) and continuing to the present day, one man has set an example of giving to Governor Dummer Academy which has not only, in itself, provided for vast and greatly needed capital improvements, but which has spurred most generous donations by others. For many years this man, at his own request, remained anonymous. At the dedication of the Alumni Gymnasium in June, 1950, however, Mr. Eames for the first time identified him as Mr. Morris P. Frost, a member of the Class of 1935.

Mr. Frost a few years after his graduation from the Academy gave evidence of a desire to help the school in any way he could. From the first, his gifts have been given unpretentiously and so as to serve the best interests of Governor Dummer. Elected a member of the Board in 1947, when in 1949 it appeared that the school could afford to build neither the projected alumni gymnasium nor the classroom building, he subordinated his own wishes and contributed heavily to the construction of the former.

In January, 1955, however, Morris Frost renewed his offer to provide for the erection of a new classroom building, the most serious current need of the Academy. His gift of $425,000 was to pay the full cost of construction. The Trustees set up a committee, under the chairmanship of Mr. Philip Morgan, to raise an additional $225,000 for the purpose of furnishing and equipping this new library and science building. The total fund, therefore, including Mr. Frost's gift, was to amount to $650,000.

In June, 1956, workmen started the task of raising and moving Perkins Dormitory to its new location on Middle Road, across the way from the Alumni Gymnasium. (This was the second move for the main part of that venerable building, which had originally been the school gymnasium, erected near the Mansion House in 1887.) Already, as the result of long hours of work by the committee and through the generosity of nearly 700 friends, both old and new, the fund drive had almost achieved its goal.

On Parents Day, October 19, 1957, with the fund oversubscribed by $22,000, the beautiful new Library and Science Building was formally dedicated and named in honor of Morris Pratt Frost. Even with the completion of this newest campus structure, surely one of the finest and most functional school buildings in New England, Mr. Frost's important gifts to Governor Dummer Academy were not to end.

Much has been said throughout this history about the decisions and acts of the Board of Trustees, but relatively little about the men who have made up the Board. A list of those with ten years or more of service appears in the Appendix; it is unfortunate that but a little more can here be said of their individual contributions, especially in the cases of those men whose efforts and judgment have been instrumental over the past thirty years in the building of the present school.

The recent Trustees have counted in their number distinguished men, honored for their work in a wide variety of fields. For thirty-nine years a member of the Board, from June, 1916, until his resignation in June, 1955, Dr. Arthur W. Ewell had been awarded in 1946 an honorary Doctor of Science degree from Worcester Polytechnic Institute, where he was a renowned teacher. William S. Nutter, manufacturing consultant and inventor, who resigned from the Board in 1954, in 1949 had received an honorary Doctor of

Science degree from the University of Maine. Dr. Boyden of Deerfield Academy has been recognized with honorary doctorates by numerous colleges and universities, including Harvard, Dartmouth, and Tufts. Likewise a recipient of doctorates from Dartmouth and Tufts, Dr. Fuess has been honored by five other universities as well. In 1947 Dr. Arthur W. Allen, formerly President of the American College of Surgeons, was appointed a Fellow of the Royal College of Surgeons in London. Dr. Allen remained on the Board until his death in March, 1958. Mr. Marshall B. Dalton, successor to Mr. Phillips as President of the Governor Dummer Board of Trustees, in 1957 was made a Fellow of the American Academy of Arts and Sciences, and in 1958 was awarded an honorary doctorate in Engineering by the Worcester Polytechnic Institute. Elected a Trustee of Governor Dummer three years earlier, the Reverend Mr. George L. Cadigan was honored in 1958 by his alma mater, Amherst College, with an honorary Doctor of Divinity degree, then in 1959 elevated in the Protestant Episcopal Church to the position of Bishop of Missouri. James Duncan Phillips, dedicated President of the Board from 1933 until his death in 1954, a Trustee and benefactor from 1924, was chosen an honorary member of the Harvard University chapter of Phi Beta Kappa in 1947. Duncan Phillips insured that even after his death the Academy to which he had given unstintingly of his time, energy, and money for more than thirty years would continue to benefit from his interest, for Governor Dummer appeared as one of the chief beneficiaries under his will.

Mr. Phillips's interest in the Academy was not only genuine and deep, but entirely natural, growing out of his consuming love of New England Yankee tradition and things old, especially when "that tradition and those things old embody things worth preserving." His service to the school was momentous. Upon the election of his successor in January, 1955, the Board strove to characterize some of Duncan Phillips's contributions in these words:

> . . .To Governor Dummer Academy, as President of the Board of Trustees, Mr. Phillips gave the devotion of his later years, and no school has ever had a more intelligent patron and friend. He watched jealously over its interests, paid attention to even the smallest details of management, brought it to the public notice whenever possible, and guarded well its finances and scholastic reputation. His benefactions to the school, continuing

even after his death, placed him among the enlightened philanthropists of his time. . .

It is difficult to pass over the services of many other such loyal Trustees as Leon M. Little, eighteen years on the Board, its Treasurer when Mr. Eames came to the school and for more than ten years thereafter; or as David Wheatland, twenty-four years a Trustee, long-time Secretary of the Finance Committee, faithful and interested throughout his entire association with the school. There remains space only, however, to characterize, and then but sparsely, the personnel of the Board during the last part of Mr. Eames's tenure — in whose hands rested so much affecting the future conduct of the Academy.

Those whose associations with the school are already familiar to the reader include — with the dates of their election to the Board — Dr. Frank L. Boyden (1929), Dr. Claude M. Fuess (1933), Morris P. Frost (1947), Roger B. Coulter (1949), and the Right Reverend George L. Cadigan (1955). In addition, President of the Trustees since January, 1955, has been Marshall B. Dalton, a warm, direct, keen-minded executive who is Chairman of the Boards of both the Boston Manufacturers Mutual Insurance Company and the Mutual Boiler and Machinery Insurance Company. He is, as well, a life member of the Corporation of the Massachusetts Institute of Technology, and a member of its Executive and Finance Committees. A Trustee on the Governor Dummer Board since 1940, he served as its Treasurer during the years of its greatest financial and physical growth, until elected Vice-President in June, 1954. The last twenty years in the school's history are dotted with countless undertakings requiring everything from diplomacy to a decisive action — and to the successful accomplishment of which Mr. Dalton has quietly and effectively directed his talents.

Listed in order of their election, the following Trustees have joined their efforts and their particular insights to those of the six already mentioned, greatly to the profit of the Academy.

Senior to all but Doctors Boyden and Fuess, in terms of length of service, Lispenard B. Phister (cited for leadership by Trinity College in 1955) has been a Trustee since 1938. In his capacity as Secretary of the Board since 1948, he is responsible for the incisive and often witty records of recent Trustee meetings, which have become indispensable to this writer.

Vice-President of the Board Philip M. Morgan, elected in 1942, has from the first been a moving force behind the Academy's expansion program, often devoting much of his time to the raising of funds important to its plans. A Worcester, Massachusetts, businessman and community leader, chairman of the Board of Trustees and holder of an honorary doctorate at Worcester Polytechnic Institute, he has seen two sons graduate from Governor Dummer.

Academy Treasurer since 1945, Augustus P. Loring, of Boston, a professional trustee, serves as a director of many business and charitable corporations. Mr. Loring joined the Board in 1951 and has since been one of its most active members.

Gerry J. Dietz is the vigorous and energetic President of the R. E. Dietz Company of Syracuse, New York. In 1952 he became the third of the triumvirate of Governor Dummer graduates on the Board, joining Messrs. Frost and Coulter. (It is said that at a Trustees meeting shortly after a hurricane had wrought considerable damage to the electrical circuit at the Academy, Mr. Dietz alertly seized the opportunity to apprise his colleagues of the fact that there is nothing like Dietz kerosene lanterns for dependable lighting!)

Elected to the Board with the Reverend Cadigan in 1955 was Allen Davidson, active businessman of Boston, formerly President of the Boston Retail Trade Board, whose close interest in the school dated from prior to his son's graduation at Byfield in 1951.

Finally, elected within five months of each other (in November, 1956, and April, 1957) are Frederick S. Moseley, Jr., of New York and Lothrop Withington of Boston. Both of these men, through their forebears, have a remarkable history of association with the Academy. Mr. Moseley's father had been a graduate of the school; his great grandfather, grandfather, and uncle had given, among them, almost a century of service as Trustees. Great grandson of the Reverend Leonard Withington, a leading Trustee during the second quarter of the last century, Lothrop Withington is also the son of a Trustee and the father of three Governor Dummer graduates. Finally, he is related to two more graduates and to a former faculty member.

*   *   *   *   *

This is a special year on the campus because four of the men whom I brought with me, when I came here in the summer of 1930, are now completing their twenty-fifth consecutive year of teaching at Governor Dummer. These men are Edgar Dunning, Thomas Mercer, Macdonald Murphy, and Arthur Sager . . . These four men,

working with me and with each other, have provided the
foundation upon which the school, as we know it today,
has been built, and they continue even now to carry on
their shoulders the framework of the Academy. Where
is there another school so fortunate?

Thus, in part, read Mr. Eames's letter to the Alumni at the beginning of the *Alumni Bulletin* for Spring, 1955. The remarkable
record of the Headmaster and his four colleagues during the twenty-
five years of their association with the school, and the impact which
they had had upon the boys who studied under them, were
reflected in the many occasions upon which they were honored
during the years 1954-55. At the crowded Alumni dinner, held in
their honor at the Harvard Club in February, each member of the
"Old Guard" had his moment as the target of reminiscence and
the object of esteem.

In 1957 Ben Stone reached his twenty-fifth year as a member of
the Governor Dummer Faculty. In 1961 Howard Navins passed
that same milestone, and at the same time Roy Ohrn entered his
20th year. In his 1955 letter to the Alumni Mr. Eames had said:
"We do not forget that there are many other loyal and devoted
teachers . . . many other veteran friends of the school . . ." Indeed,
excellent young teachers have come over the years to Governor
Dummer and stayed on; a whole new generation has blended into
the life of the school, becoming an important element in one of the
main strengths of the venerable Academy today, its faculty. Yet
surely, that the core of this strength should be comprised of eight
men who have lived and worked together so successfully toward
the same end for an aggregate total of almost 200 years must be
very nearly unique in the annals of private education in this
country.

In July, 1958, friends of the school everywhere received a letter
from Mr. Eames himself, containing the startling announcement
of his projected retirement, to be effective on July 1 of the following
summer. The letter was received with surprise, regret, and yet with
pride. For here was ending a career in which a whole new destiny
had been shaped for an old and honored school, shaped in a very
large degree by the complete dedication and the wisdom of its
Headmaster. In twenty-six years at the helm of the Academy,
Master Moody built a legend; Dr. Ingham gave twenty-three years
of single-minded and sincere service. Upon retiring Dr. Eames
would be bringing to completion the longest period of leadership
in the history of the school, twenty-nine years of amazing growth

Edmund Kelly - Boston Globe

"THE OLD GUARD" (1955) :

A. Macdonald Murphy, Edgar D. Dunning, Edward W. Eames,
Thomas McC. Mercer, Arthur W. Sager

and development. "I am proud of what all of us working together over the years have accomplished," wrote the Headmaster in his letter:

> When I say *all of us,* I mean to include a great many of you good friends of the school, as well as the faculty, trustees, and alumni. I believe that today Governor Dummer is stronger, its morale higher, its reputation better, than at any time since I have been associated with the school. I would like to be able to step aside when things are going well and to resist the temptation to stay a little too long. For personal reasons, too, it would be pleasant to lay down the burden while I am still able to hobble up and down the precipitous slopes of the Ould Newbury golf course.

"Dr. Eames has been much more than a stereotyped headmaster." So begins the "critical appraisal" written for the *Alumni Bulletin* of 1959 by Dr. Fuess:

> He has met well the conventional requirements, but he has also an individual quality of his own; and the school which is now so definitely *his* is no imitation of any other . . . It may fairly be said of Eames that he has been the ideal person to revitalize the historic school, to give it new character and power in the light of contemporary needs, to carry it triumphantly through depression and war and prosperity, and to leave it almost unrecognizable by anyone familiar with it thirty years ago, stamped with his personality and equipped to meet new contingencies and problems. . .

Only those who have worked with Ted Eames can truly comprehend the quality of painstaking and patient leadership that has gone into the designing of the school over the period of nearly three decades. Energy and precision and thought, these, together with unstinting devotion to the myriad aspects of school administration, of educating boys, have been his gift to Governor Dummer. Thousands of hours of careful concentration have been devoted to guiding young men toward wise selection concerning colleges, or to the exhaustive and detailed consideration of every phase of construction and use in the planning of new buildings, or to the most constructive move to be made next in the best interests of the school — it is impossible to encompass, even in general terms, all the facets that have had the full and ungrudging attention of the Headmaster.

Yet this work at the school, done with the steadfast and wise support of Mrs. Eames, has been only part of Mr. Eames's effort. Realizing that no school can succeed by sequestering itself within narrow corridors leading to its own "Ivory Tower," he threw himself with equal vigor into community and alumni activities, as well as the work of service organizations in Education such as the Headmasters Association (of which he was elected President in 1957). As reported regularly in *The Archon,* the Headmaster's calendar was customarily crowded with speaking engagements; alumni dinners; Trustee meetings at other institutions, such as his alma mater, Amherst; meetings of the Essex County YMCA Committee, with which he was associated for many years and to which the Academy played host annually; meetings of the Corporation of the Anna Jaques Hospital in Newburyport; or of such education groups as the College Entrance Examination Board and the New England Association of Colleges and Secondary Schools.

The amount of time devoted to the job was enormous — and the job accomplished was not merely the continuing of Governor Dummer Academy as the oldest boys' boarding school in America, but the constituting of it as one of the very best as well. In honoring Mr. Eames during the Commencement Dinner ending the Headmaster's twenty-fifth year at the school, Dr. Charles Cole, President of Amherst College, said it succinctly:

> . . .in a remarkable fashion — for a quarter of a century — Ted Eames with the faculty he has gathered here has been realizing the special potentialities of the independent school.
>
> He has brought to Governor Dummer the vitality of aspiration and the satisfaction of success.

As Ted Eames completed his final year at the head of the Academy, the significance of his achievement, as understood and appreciated by the school's thousands of alumni and friends, was reflected once again in a generous gift for the construction of a sorely needed athletic field and track. David E. Huggins, a member of the Class of 1939 and a former holder of the Academy high jump record, made the gift, together with his mother, as a memorial to his father, the late G. Ellsworth Huggins of Montclair, New Jersey. Thus Dr. Eames was leaving a school which was still growing — which, so largely due to his efforts, had earned the support and enthusiasm of an increasing number of alumni and friends. He was leaving behind him even more than this, however.

Stronger than the proud buildings, wider than the broad expanse of playing fields, even sounder than the patiently won endowment — beyond all of these he was leaving an educational institution of the first magnitude.

EPILOGUE

In September, 1958, Marshall Dalton, at the request of the Trustees, became the Chairman of the committee to choose the new Headmaster for Governor Dummer. He appointed to work with him Doctors Boyden and Fuess and Messrs. Davidson, Morgan and Moseley. Dr. Eames, expressing full confidence in such a committee, had indicated his desire to stand aside while it considered candidates to succeed him.

Working as a team, the members sought advice and suggestions from a wide variety of sources. Members of the Academy faculty were contacted and their points of view solicited. Each member of the "Old Guard" was interviewed, individually and at length, by the Chairman. To each of their opinions the Committee gave special attention. Thus the Trustees were able to avail themselves of the best advice and the fullest cooperation of all those whose judgments they valued most. As in their deliberations they narrowed the field of eligible candidates, they invited certain of the men under consideration, with their wives, to visit the Academy in order to talk with the members of the selection committee, view the school, and meet the boys and the faculty. Four final candidates were invited to revisit the Academy and to talk again with the Committee. Mr. Dalton and others of the group paid visits to the men on their home grounds. After five months of diligent search and study, the Committee was faced with the difficult task of arriving at a final recommendation to the full Board. Its decision — and that of the whole board—was enthusiastic and unanimous. On January 17, 1959, Mr. Dalton announced the selection: Mr. Valleau Wilkie, Jr., who was, at thirty-five years of age, completing his eleventh year on the faculty at Phillips Academy, Andover. There is a particular rightness in the fact that the school to which the Academy had almost 200 years before sent Samuel Phillips, its founder, and Eliphalet Pearson, its first principal, should thus return the favor.

Although Val Wilkie has said that, until approached by Governor Dummer, he had never seriously thought of assuming the responsibilities of a headmaster, it is difficult to conceive how the Committee could have settled upon a man more perfectly fitted for the job. Dr. Eames once characterized the Board's choice of Mr. Dalton to "chair" the selection committee by saying, "The Trustees stepped

168

Bachrach
JAMES DUNCAN PHILLIPS

Fabian Bachrach
MARSHALL B. DALTON

EDWARD W. EAMES

VALLEAU WILKIE, JR.

right up to bat and hit a homerun." In seeking out and getting Val Wilkie, Mr. Dalton and his committee had continued to bat 1.000.

On several occasions during the remainder of the school year 1958-1959, Mr. and Mrs. Wilkie came to Governor Dummer to meet the boys, the faculty and faculty wives under more normal conditions. The headmaster-to-be was guest of honor at a dinner with the Executive Committee of the Alumni Association. During the first weeks of the summer, Dr. Eames worked closely with his successor, to make the handing over of the reins occur as smoothly as possible. Thus a new chapter in the history of the school was begun.

What a determined young man coming to South Byfield in 1930 had done for the school in the three decades that followed must naturally have stood in the forefront of the Trustees' minds as they pondered the matter of his successor. To fill the spot they had chosen another young man, one with a different, though equally impressive background. Dr. John Kemper, Andover's Headmaster, speaking about Mr. Wilkie on the occasion of his official installation as the twenty-fourth Headmaster of the Academy summed up his value as a school man by ascribing to him enthusiasm, leadership and administrative savvy, competitive spirit and openmindedness — and, perhaps most significantly, high standards and humanity.

Son of an independent school headmaster, Val Wilkie has a Bachelor of Arts degree from Yale, and a Master of Arts in History from Harvard. His career at Yale was interrupted by the war. His three year tour of duty as an Army Air Corps bomber pilot was tough and unrelenting, ending in twelve months spent first, with the aid of the Dutch underground, dodging the Germans, then as a prisoner of war of the Nazis.

Having been a successful football player at Yale, he later achieved notable success as a coach at Andover. More important, however, was his work as a teacher and a leader of boys. It is clear from all evidence — by the boys, his Headmaster, his colleagues at Andover — that Val Wilkie was a very great deal more than simply a classroom teacher. He was that, indeed, with real distinction. But more, he reflected a quiet, sure sense of purpose, a mature judgment, a general quality of excellence which gained him that respect and affection which must go hand in hand where the true teacher and leader of boys is concerned.

Dr. Kemper had focused upon one other major qualification: the fact that accompanying Mr. Wilkie to Governor Dummer would be his wife, the former Marjorie Hankin, a graduate of Mount Holyoke College. Mrs. Wilkie had from the first been received at the Academy with the same appreciaton and enthusiasm as her husband. — And there was one more good omen: the Wilkies would bring with them to the Mansion House two children, a daughter Janice and a son Robert, making them the fifth consecutive Headmaster and wife (beginning with Perley Horne) to have one girl and one boy.

In handing the reins over to Mr. Wilkie, Dr. Eames expressed himself as particularly proud of the faculty which had been with him at the school during his last year — proud of them as a team and proud that almost to a man they were returning under his successor. With the opening of the next school year, the new Headmaster wasted no time rolling up his sleeves and getting down to business. ". . .This is no time to congratulate ourselves on a job well done," he wrote in the November *Archon,* having alluded to the position which the school had achieved in the front rank of independent schools. "In these days, to stand still is to fall behind, and only by running can one continue to gain ground." It became clear that under Val Wilkie the emphasis at Governor Dummer would remain to draw from each boy the best that is in him, to question, to confront, to challenge him — to set up a tough program, tempered by understanding, in all areas of school life. But one note of caution from the new Headmaster spoke clearly of the prime obligation of the Academy:

> Even if the Academy carries out all of the other parts of its job well, failure to instill in students a sense of obligation to their society and to themselves means failure to carry out a vital part of our function.

*   *   *   *   *

Val Wilkie views his responsibilities for the future primarily as being obligations to people. The door to his office in the Phillips Building is open to students, faculty, and friends of the school who have reason to see him. Partly to make himself as accessible as possible and partly because of his firm belief in team-effort, he has delegated widely, both to faculty and to boys, many of the responsibilities for keeping the wheels of the Academy running smoothly, retaining always the right of consultation and review. The "sense of obligation" to self and to others, of which he has spoken, is as essential in the life of the school as in life outside.

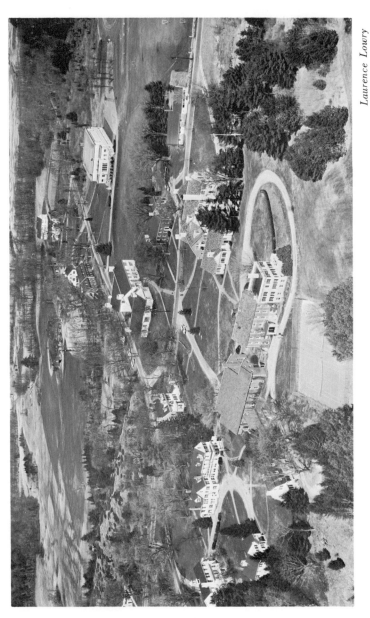

GOVERNOR DUMMER ACADEMY — AERIAL VIEW, 1961
Looking northwest toward the salt marshes and the Parker River

Laurence Lowry

The growth of the school continues unabated, physically, intellectually, and spiritually. Through the continued generosity of Morris Frost, a new artificial ice rink has been constructed to eliminate the uncertain effects of weather for scores of hockey and ice-skating enthusiasts during the long winters. The venerable Moody Boynton House across Middle Road, near Perkins and the Alumni Gymnasium, has been beautifully restored to provide an attractive faculty apartment and rooms for several boys. This fine old Colonial home, purchased by the Board in 1951, has a long and honorable history of association with the Academy, having in earlier days won renown as the boarding house run by Deacon Daniel Hale. In January, 1960, the Trustees elected to a vacancy in their membership Elliott M. Gordon, veteran engineer and industrialist, recently brought to the Presidency of the Towle Manufacturing Company of Newburyport. Mr. Gordon, formerly a Sloan Fellow at M. I. T., holds an honorary E. D. from Purdue University. In June of that year, Mr. Wilkie was likewise welcomed as a full-fledged member of the Board. The academic program of the school, as well as all other phases, continues to undergo thoughtful scrutiny. In the desire to supply another important area of guidance to the students, a school chaplain has been appointed; there are plans in the future for a chapel on campus.

There are many other plans as well, all calculated to build upon the strengths of the Academy. The focus for the future is to keep in the school a vital and dynamic force and spirit, capable of meeting and fulfilling with increasing success the challenge of the rapidly expanding and complex universe of mankind.

The question has been asked, If at any one evil stroke every independent school in the country were to be totally destroyed, what justification might be advanced for plans to re-establish that medium of education? For of the entire secondary school population, only about 2% attend independent schools.

That there *is* ample justification, we who have been associated with such schools are convinced. There are, furthermore, few in the field of public education who would wish to take issue with the fact. Yet it is evident beyond doubt that no privately endowed academy can afford complacently to open its doors merely as a refuge for those who, for whatever reason, turn their backs on the public schools. The effective independent school conscientiously builds and maintains a program derived from a deep sense of purpose, based on a genuine conviction of obligation to the society which it serves — the kind of obligation which it can serve best because, through its independence of thought and action, it can best gird itself to the task.

In 1763 Lieutenant Governor Dummer's vision of a school which would provide the education so important and so hard to come by in his day and place became a vigorous reality. Now, 200 years later, Governor Dummer Academy, never more vigorous, has taken its stand in the first rank of those institutions for which it was the prototype. Though 200 years old, the Academy is in the young manhood of its strength, poised to take up its responsibilities at the outset of a new era of challenge and of service.

THE APPENDIX

The Original Trustees

(In Accordance with the
Will of Lieutenant Governor William Dummer)
The Reverend Mr. Thomas Foxcroft
The Reverend Dr. Charles Chauncey
Mr. Nathaniel Dummer

The First Board of Trustees
(In Accordance with the Act of Incorporation, 1782)
Honorable Jeremiah Powell, President
Honorable Benjamin Greenleaf, Vice-President
The Reverend Moses Parsons, Secretary
Nathaniel Tracy, Treasurer
The Reverend Joseph Willard
The Reverend Dr. Charles Chauncey
Honorable Jonathan Greenleaf
The Reverend John Tucker
The Reverend Thomas Cary
Samuel Moody, Master
William Powell
Micajah Sawyer
Dummer Jewett
Samuel Osgood
Richard Dummer

The Present Board of Trustees of Governor Dummer Academy
1961
Marshall B. Dalton, President
Philip M. Morgan, Vice-President
Lispenard B. Phister, Secretary
Augustus P. Loring, Treasurer
Frank L. Boyden
The Right Reverend George L. Cadigan
Roger B. Coulter
Allen Davidson
Gerry J. Dietz
Morris P. Frost
Claude Moore Fuess
Elliott M. Gordon
Frederick S. Moseley, Jr.
Valleau Wilkie, Jr.
Lothrop Withington

173

Governor Dummer Academy Headmasters, 1763-1961

Samuel Moody	1763 - 1790
Isaac Smith	1790 - 1809
Benjamin Allen	1809 - 1811
Abiel Abbot	1811 - 1819
Samuel Adams	1819 - 1821
Nehemiah Cleaveland	1821 - 1840
Phineas Nichols	1837 - 1840
(English Department)	(Remained briefly after 1840 as Assistant)
Frederic A. Adams	1840 - 1846
Henry Durant	1847 - 1849
Ariel Parish Chute	1850 - 1852
Marshall Henshaw	1853 - 1859
John S. Parsons	1861 - 1862
Solon Albee	1863 - 1864
Edwin L. Foster	**1864**
Levi Wentworth Stanton	1866 - 1872
Ebenezer Greenleaf Parsons	1872 - 1882
John Wright Perkins	1882 - 1894
George B. Rogers	1894 - 1896
Perley Leonard Horne	1896 - 1904
William Dudley Sprague	1904 - 1906
Leon E. Ryther	1906 - 1907
Charles S. Ingham	1907 - 1930
Edward W. Eames	1930 - 1959
Valleau Wilkie, Jr.	1959 -

Names and Terms of Men Serving Ten Years or Longer as
Trustees of Governor Dummer Academy

Charles Chauncey	1761 - 1789*
Benjamin Greenleaf	1782 - 1798
Joseph Willard	1782 - 1804
Jonathan Greenleaf	1782 - 1806
John Tucker	1782 - 1792
Thomas Cary	1782 - 1808
Micajah Sawyer	1782 - 1815
Richard Dummer	1782 - 1805
Theophilus Bradbury	1784 - 1803
Theophilus Parsons	1784 - 1813
Joseph Hale	1786 - 1817
John Andrews	1789 - 1838
William Coombs	1789 - 1814
John Adams	1792 - 1804
Ebenezer March	1797 - 1819
Elijah Parish	1797 - 1825
Nathaniel Carter	1800 - 1818
John Snelling Popkin	1806 - 1822
Eben Parsons	1806 - 1819
Daniel White	1809 - 1820
Silas Little	1809 - 1827
Dudley Atkins Tyng	1815 - 1828
Daniel Hale	1815 - 1837
Ebenezer Moseley	1815 - 1840
James Morss	1818 - 1833
Samuel S. Wilde	1820 - 1830
Nathan Noyes	1822 - 1832
Jeremiah Nelson	1825 - 1838
Moses Dole	1826 - 1847
Daniel Adams	1828 - 1866
Jeremiah Colman	1829 - 1866
Leonard Withington, (served two terms)	1831 - 1838
	1846 - 1852

*The other two original Trustees under the Governor's Will, The Reverend Thomas Foxcroft and Mr. Nathaniel Dummer, died prior to the passing of the Act of Incorporation.

Thomas B. Fox	1833 - 1850
John C. March	1833 - 1847
Jonathan G. Johnson	1833 - 1853
Henry Durant	1834 - 1847
Daniel Noyes	1837 - 1868
David Choate	1840 - 1850
John Pike	1843 - 1895
Asahel Huntington	1846 - 1870
Benjamin A. Gould	1848 - 1859
David S. Caldwell	1851 - 1883
Edward S. Moseley	1852 - 1900
Daniel Fitz	1853 - 1869
Allen W. Dodge	1853 - 1865
Luther Moody	1853 - 1871
Samuel G. Spalding	1857 - 1892
Benjamin A. Gould (the son)	1860 - 1894
Dean Peabody	1866 - 1882
Daniel P. Noyes	1866 - 1888
Moses Colman	1870 - 1900
George A. Todd	1870 - 1883
George F. Choate	1872 - 1888
Joseph S. Dodge	1874 - 1903
William Dummer Northend	1876 - 1901
Robert Codman	1876 - 1900
Charles W. Moseley	1883 - 1908
Alexander B. Forbes	1885 - 1895
Isaac C. Wyman	1888 - 1910
John Hamilton Morse (served two terms)	1890 - 1907
	1916 - 1928
John W. Candler	1890 - 1903
Egbert Coffin Smythe	1892 - 1904
David C. Torrey	1893 - 1911
Edward P. Noyes	1895 - 1913
Edmund H. Stevens	1895 - 1905
Fred M. Ambrose	1895 - 1931
James Hardy Ropes	1898 - 1909
John Peirce	1900 - 1934
Jarvis Lamson	1903 - 1924
Alden P. White	1903 - 1933
Edward B. George	1903 - 1913
Joseph N. Dummer	1906 - 1942
Charles S. Ingham	1908 - 1922
	1924 - 1930

Frederick P. Cabot	1909 - 1924
Alfred A. Ordway	1909 - 1920
Glenn Tilley Morse	1913 - 1950
Arthur W. Ewell	1916 - 1955
Laurence P. Dodge	1917 - 1931
Roland H. Sherman	1918 - 1929
Frederick H. Goodwin	1920 - 1949
William A. Lang	1922 - 1937
James Duncan Phillips	1924 - 1954
Leon M. Little	1929 - 1947
Frank L. Boyden	1930 -
David P. Wheatland	1932 - 1956
Claude Moore Fuess	1933 -
Edward W. Eames	1934 - 1959
Arthur W. Allen	1938 - 1958
Lispenard B. Phister	1938 -
Marshall B. Dalton	1940 -
William Nutter	1940 - 1954
Philip M. Morgan	1942 -
Morris P. Frost	1947 -
Roger B. Coulter	1949 -
Augustus P. Loring	1951

INDEX

(This Index does not include reference to listings in Appendix)

INDEX (Continued)

INDEX (Continued)

INDEX (Continued)

INDEX (Concluded)